Comments on other *Amazing Stories* from readers & reviewers

"Tightly written volumes filled with lots of wit and humour about famous and infamous Canadians."
Eric Shackleton, *The Globe and Mail*

"The heightened sense of drama and intrigue, combined with a good dose of human interest is what sets Amazing Stories *apart."*
Pamela Klaffke, *Calgary Herald*

"This is popular history as it should be... For this price, buy two and give one to a friend."
Terry Cook, a reader from Ottawa, on *Rebel Women*

"Glasner creates the moment of the explosion itself in graphic detail...she builds detail upon gruesome detail to create a convincingly authentic picture."
Peggy McKinnon, *The Sunday Herald*, on *The Halifax Explosion*

"It was wonderful...I found I could not put it down. I was sorry when it was completed."
Dorothy F. from Manitoba on *Marie-Anne Lagimodière*

"Stories are rich in description, and bristle with a clever, stylish realness."
Mark Weber, *Central Alberta Advisor*, on *Ghost Town Stories II*

"A compelling read. Bertin...has selected only the most intriguing tales, which she narrates with a wealth of detail."
Joyce Glasner, *New Brunswick Reader*, on *Strange Events*

"The resulting book is one readers will want to share with all the women in their lives."
Lynn Martel, *Rocky Mountain Outlook*, on *Women Explorers*

AMAZING STORIES®

MARY SCHÄFFER

AMAZING STORIES®

MARY SCHÄFFER

An Adventurous Woman's
Exploits in the Canadian Rockies

HISTORY/BIOGRAPHY
by Jill Foran

PUBLISHED BY ALTITUDE PUBLISHING CANADA LTD.
1500 Railway Avenue, Canmore, Alberta T1W 1P6
www.altitudepublishing.com
1-800-957-6888

Publisher	Stephen Hutchings
Associate Publisher	Kara Turner
Editor	Lori Burwash

We acknowledge the financial support of the Government
of Canada through the Book Publishing Industry Development
Program (BPIDP) for our publishing activities.

Altitude GreenTree Program
Altitude Publishing will plant twice as many trees as were
used in the manufacturing of this product.

National Library of Canada Cataloguing in Publication Data
Foran, Jill
  Mary Schäffer: an adventurous woman's exploits in the Canadian Rockies
/ Jill Foran

(Amazing stories)
Includes bibliographical references.
ISBN 1-55153-999-3

1. Schäffer, Mary T. S. (Mary Townsend Sharples), 1861-1939. 2. Rocky
Mountains, Canadian (B.C. and Alta)--Biography.* 3. Explorers--Rocky
Mountains, Canadian (B.C. and Alta)--Biography.* I. Title. II Series:
Amazing stories (Canmore, Alta.)
FC218.S32F67 2003   971.1'03'092   C2003-910077-4
F1090.F67 2003

Printed and bound in Canada by Friesen Printers
4 6 8 9 7 5

To the pioneering women of western
Canada, whose adventurous spirits
are an inspiration to this day

Mary Schäffer and Billy Warren

Contents

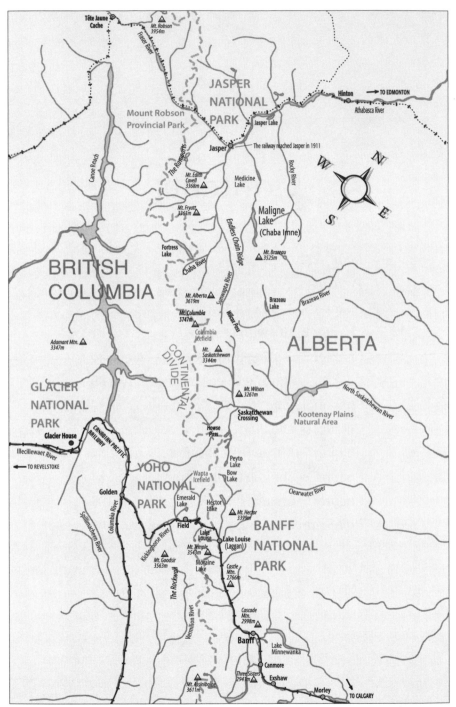

A map of the Rocky Mountains between Morley and Tête Jaune Cache

Prologue

July 4, 1908. It was probably the coldest fourth of July Mary had ever known. It came with biting winds and freezing rain, and it was assaulting the whole outfit with no mercy. Mary's high spirits were wavering. It was Independence Day, after all, and here she was, somewhere in the Canadian Rockies, hunched on a horse and shielding her face from the elements.

Back home, people were having picnics and setting off fireworks. Back home, her family and friends were sweating in the stifling summer heat of Philadelphia. If they could see her now, they would assail her with I told you so's. Few of them had wanted her to go on this quest. They thought it foolish and unladylike. But they had no idea of the beauty and the peace and the freedom she had found in the wilderness. And they did not have a map to a secret lake, a lake that lay hidden deep in the mountains, just waiting to be discovered. Mary had a map.

Perched on her horse, high atop a mountain pass, Mary watched her guide work to clear burnt timber from their slippery trail. Then she glanced at Mollie and the others. They all looked cold and miserable in their slickers and ponchos. Were they silently cursing her? Perhaps they had a right. After all, she had pushed the hardest for this expedition. She had sought out the map and paid for the guides, the horses, and the gear.

Now they were almost one month into the search, freezing and disheartened, and apparently nowhere near their destination. No one, not even the team's leader, was sure that the route they had chosen was the right one. Mary was not sure where they were at all. But despite the weather and the questionable trail, despite the doubts and increasing bickering, Mary was sure of one thing: come hell or high water, they would find this lake.

Chapter 1

A Rebel Is Born

ary Sharples was four years old when she first deliberately broke a rule. Until that day, she knew little about the world beyond her home. Her young life consisted of parents and brothers, nannies and maids, playtime and bedtime. A precocious child, Mary could already read and write, so her father was careful when selecting her "first books." Of course, the girl never questioned her father's choices. Belonging to a strict Quaker family, Mary was taught that children were to obey their parents. For the most part, she abided by that rule, never questioning authority.

One summer evening, things changed when Mary was

introduced to a world beyond her wildest imagination. It came in the form of a visitor, a distant relative whom she was gently instructed to call Cousin Jim. Mary was mesmerized by the strange man standing in her parents' library — Cousin Jim was nothing like her other relatives. He was an officer in the United States Army, and he wore a uniform that screamed of authority and adventure. Mary was in awe of the brass buttons, the golden epaulettes, and the clanking spurs. Wide-eyed, she watched as this astonishing figure visited with her suddenly uninteresting family.

Mary's reverie was broken when she was sent off to eat supper and go to bed. Not wanting to miss a moment of Cousin Jim's visit, she began to concoct a naughty plan as her nurse unceremoniously led her away. Once alone in her nursery, Mary slipped out of the room, dragging a child-sized stool behind her. She crept to the veranda and set the small seat in a quiet, dark corner where no one would see her. There she hid, hoping that after the grown-ups had finished their dinner, they would retire outside to enjoy the warm night.

After what seemed like a great deal of waiting, the adults emerged and settled on the veranda, where the men lit cigars and sighed contentedly. Mary slouched on her stool, trying her best to be invisible in the darkness of the vines. At first, the conversation was disappointing to the young spy. Talk focussed on other relatives and the politics of the day. But just as Mary was getting bored — and annoyed — Cousin Jim began to talk of his life in the West. Finally, the conversation was getting good.

Jim spoke of forts and soldiers, buffalo hunts and animal hides, prairie schooners and long journeys across the plains. Hanging on his every word, Mary felt she was on her own adventure as she learned more about this place so different from her surroundings.

But after a while, Mary's excitement turned to fear. Oblivious that young ears were listening, Jim described an experience that had left him traumatized. Having come upon a native village that had just been destroyed by fellow soldiers, Jim was moved by the scene of devastation. Many men, women, and children lay murdered around him. Looking at the bodies strewn about, Jim noticed that beneath one woman's corpse lay a crying baby. Feeling sick, he picked up the child, discovering that its face had been splattered with its mother's blood.

Unable to listen to the tale any longer, Mary cried out. Cousin Jim immediately stopped talking, and Mary's mother rushed to the corner. She yanked the girl off her stool and called the nanny, who led an ashamed and frightened Mary away. Once in the nursery, she cried and cried for the baby who had lost its mother to such a terrible death.

That night, four-year-old Mary's life changed dramatically. Not only had she experienced her first taste of rebellion, she had also begun to think of life beyond her familiar surroundings. Mary wanted to see new places and be among different people. From that night on, she always asked to hear tales of life in the West, and she constantly sought out stories of the peoples of the plains. This obsession with native culture and distant lands lasted through her childhood.

* * *

Mary Townsend Sharples was born on October 4, 1861. She grew up in West Chester, Pennsylvania, a large borough just west of Philadelphia. Her parents, Alfred and Elizabeth Sharpless (they spelled their name with a double 's'), were prominent residents of the community. Both were descended from wealthy Quaker families and, like their parents and grandparents before them, were heavily involved in the borough's religious activities, as well as its social ones. Alfred worked for many years as the superintendent of transportation at the Schuylkill Navigation Company. In 1870, he left that position, returning to his farming roots and dabbling in politics.

Alfred and Elizabeth provided their five children with many comforts and advantages. The Sharpless household was always well staffed with maids, cooks, nannies, and other servants. This meant that none of the children had much to do in the way of chores. When she was six, Mary was assigned her first and only chore: watching over her younger brothers, Fred and Herman. To Mary, this was hardly work. She enjoyed mothering her siblings and was good at caring for them. She was also a good student, a fact that undoubtedly brought relief to the Quaker household, where practicality and empirical thinking were a major part of life.

School and baby-sitting made Mary happy enough, but her extracurricular activities were her real source of pleasure. Mary took art lessons throughout much of her childhood and valued the time spent learning to paint and draw. Propriety of the day demanded that she be tutored privately for such classes, so tutored she was. Alfred, having connections that extended to well-known Pennsylvania figures, hired renowned flower painter George Lambdin to teach his daughter about colour and light. Mary also loved spending time outside with her father, who was a respected amateur mineralogist, geologist, and archeologist. An avid lover of natural history, he taught Mary how to observe and catalogue nature — and that the environment should be honoured and respected.

When Mary was six, she had the privilege of getting to know one of the greatest scientists of the 19th century, Dr. Joseph Leidy, the curator of the Academy of Natural Sciences in Philadelphia. Among Leidy's many accomplishments was describing and naming *Hadrosaurus*, the first dinosaur skeleton discovered. On numerous occasions, Dr. Leidy and Alfred went for drives together in the country, taking note of interesting rocks, grasses, and plants. Being the apple of her father's eye, Mary was usually allowed to accompany the scientists. She would listen attentively as her father and the good doctor taught her tidbits of natural history. During these outdoor adventures, Mary spent as much time looking for native artifacts as she did looking at plant and rock specimens. She daydreamed of seeing the lands of the Great West, always picturing what she thought were the romantic lives of the people of the plains.

When Mary was a teenager, she finally got the opportunity to travel to the western states, when her parents took the family on a train trip to California. Beside herself with excitement, Mary could barely wait to see all her fantasies in real life: the cowboys, the native villages, the wide-open plains — everything. Now she could get a sense of the great unknown, the "uncivilized" lands and peoples that she had read and heard about for so many years. With a gleeful sense of danger, she decided to carry a small revolver in her pocket. Just to be safe.

As the train chugged through state after state, Mary realized that her ideas of the West were nothing but romantic notions — notions fed by the fictional accounts she had so eagerly read. There was no evidence of the Wild West she had dreamed about. She peered out the train window for hours at a time, her eyes combing the unfamiliar lands for teepees, horses, and Native peoples dressed in buckskin and beads. To her dismay, all she saw were ranches, cattle, and wheat field after wheat field. Would she ever see what she'd been longing for?

Not really. Mary's first glimpse of Native peoples was at a train station somewhere in the Mohave Desert. While the train was being recharged with water, a handful of passengers braved the desert's high temperature to stretch their legs. Mary was among the people to leave the train, and as she strolled up and down, she saw a group of native women standing by the station. They were not decked out in beautiful beaded jackets, nor were there any teepees in sight. Instead, Mary found herself staring at women who looked tired, hungry, and weather-beaten.

With a pang of disappointment, Mary watched as the women moved closer to the train, trying to catch pieces of tainted meat being tossed out of the dining car. Mary wondered what they would possibly do with the rotting meat. Surely they couldn't eat it. But the women rushed to a nearby muddy stream and washed the rot away. Impressed by this resourcefulness, Mary's admiration for the women soared.

Apparently, not all the passengers shared this admiration. Before anyone could stop him, a well-dressed gentleman poked one of the women with his cane. The woman spun around and threw a piece of muddy meat at her tormentor. The laughter from the train humiliated the man, and Mary felt a surge of pride at the woman's boldness. In a move that was both sisterly and courageous, she walked over to the meat thrower, caressed her shoulder, and handed her a few coins. The native woman smiled in return, making young Mary's heart take flight. During the rest of her trip, Mary had other inspiring encounters with Native peoples. Her disappointment that the West was not what she had dreamed was soon replaced by curiosity about what it actually was.

Mary's first trip across the country not only introduced her to new lands; it also planted in her an insatiable need to keep travelling. Finally she had found an outlet for her adventurous spirit, and over the next several years, she took every opportunity for travel that was offered to her. However, upon returning from her journeys, Mary often felt at a loss over what to do next. Having completed her formal education, and armed with knowledge of art, travel, and natural history, Mary wanted to do something meaningful — and different. Well aware that many of her interests were not deemed appropriate for a society lady, she could not figure out what to do with her life. A visit to the Canadian Rockies would play a major role in helping her decide.

Chapter 2

Life with Charles

I n 1889, 27-year-old Mary Sharples decided to take a trip across Canada. The Canadian Pacific Railway (CPR) had been completed only two years earlier, and wealthy tourists from near and far were eager to ride the transcontinental line. Passenger trains of the CPR were touted as utterly luxurious, boasting gourmet dining, plush sofas, and sparkling mahogany berths. The idea of travelling in such lavishness while checking out exciting new places was enough to convince Mary to embark on a journey from Montreal to Vancouver. Armed with a mental list of must-see destinations, as well as another pistol, she was ready to explore Canada.

Before Mary left for Montreal, a trusted friend told her about a charming place called Glacier House, situated high in British Columbia's Selkirk Mountains. Named for its proximity to Illecillewaet Glacier, this Swiss-style chalet was built by the CPR as a dining room and later a hotel for travellers. Because the rail grade through much of the Selkirks was steep, the trains of the day were unable to pull heavy dining cars along with the rest of the passenger cars, so the CPR developed restaurants at strategic locations. Glacier House was one of the most popular meal stops due to its pleasant décor and breathtaking scenery, and Mary had every intention of seeing it for herself.

The friend who had spoken so fondly of Glacier House was Mary Vaux, a Quaker woman close to Mary in age, who shared her love of art and travel. The Vaux family also hailed from Philadelphia and in the last few years had done a fair amount of trekking. Among their many interests were the natural sciences, and they, like the Sharplesses, had countless friends and acquaintances who shared this interest. One such friend was Dr. Charles Schäffer, a member of the Academy of Natural Sciences. Although a medical doctor by trade, Charles's true passion was botany. Upon hearing the Vauxes' descriptions of Glacier House and its fascinating flora, Charles grew increasingly eager to visit the much talked about spot.

As it turned out, Mary Sharples and Dr. Charles Schäffer crossed paths at Glacier House in 1889. Mary was introduced to the charming doctor upon disembarking from her train, and the two hit it off immediately. Despite their obvious differences — Charles was 23 years older than Mary and had been widowed twice before — their shared interest in nature left the newly acquainted twosome with much to talk about. However, Mary had planned only a brief stop at Glacier House and was disappointed when she had to abandon her new friend. She was also sad to leave such a pleasant spot so soon after she had arrived. But the Canadian Rockies had taken Mary's breath away, and she was anxious to continue her journey through the mountains.

Mary's first trip across Canada was a resounding success. Having finally seen the Canadian Rockies, she was filled with a desire to see more of them. She was also filled with a desire to see more of Dr. Schäffer, and, upon returning home to Philadelphia, Mary renewed her acquaintance with Charles. Once again they found a great deal to talk about, and a mutual attraction quickly grew — within a short time, they had fallen deeply in love and were married in a private ceremony in West Chester.

After the wedding, Mr. and Mrs. Schäffer settled into Charles's childhood home in Philadelphia. Like Mary's childhood home, this one was large and well staffed. Charles was moderately wealthy, so many of the luxuries Mary had enjoyed in West Chester were on hand in her new house. Once again, she had few household duties. This may have been a blessing, for she was not predisposed to homemaking.

Years earlier, Mary had made an effort to learn how to cook, but the resulting pie was so terrible that only her father's chickens would eat it. Her housekeeping talents were not much better. She once disclosed that she "did not know how to make a bed at the tender age of 18."

Mary's new life was more than comfortable. Charles was madly in love with his wife and showered her with gifts and attention. Belonging to several Philadelphia clubs and societies, Dr. Schäffer was among Philadelphia's elite. To Mary, this meant attending dinner parties and balls, nights at the theatre, and countless concerts. Although she willingly accompanied Charles, she often wished she were someplace else — she could not get her mind off the mountains she had journeyed through not so long ago. As Mary wrote years later, "In spite of the fact that I had entrée in the east to art circles — all that goes to make a city life adored by those who are willing to endure the black dust of rail-roads, clanging of cars twenty-four hours of the day, puddles of mud on rainy days, broiling heat of summer, etc., my heart turned to my memory pictures of the Rockies and open spaces."

Charles shared his wife's longing to see the Canadian Rockies again, and in 1891, they returned to Glacier House. The return was not purely a nostalgic one. On his first visit, Charles had made a number of exciting botanical discoveries. This time, he wanted to further research the area's flora. This trip to Glacier House marked the beginning of a long tradition. For more than a decade, the Schäffers travelled to the

Canadian Rockies each summer to study the area's flora, leaving behind Philadelphia's sweltering heat for the crisp air and wide-open spaces of the western wilderness.

Summer quickly became Mary's favourite time of year. Not only was she able to spend the sunniest months amid beautiful scenery, she could also make use of her artistic talents. At the end of a long day of collecting flora, the couple would return to Glacier House, where Mary carefully dried and pressed the specimens they had gathered. She also began to paint the flowers and plants — a gifted artist, she had an incredible ability to capture each specimen's deep colour and details, a talent that impressed her husband immensely.

Not satisfied with just drying, pressing, and painting, Mary decided that the specimens should also be photographed. Having only recently developed an interest in photography, Mary experimented with different methods in order to take the most accurate and attractive pictures possible. She then created beautiful colour slides by hand painting the negatives. The novice photographer was so successful at capturing the original hues of her subjects that her work was often exhibited in international shows. In fact, Mary's artistic contribution to the field of botany earned her a lifetime membership with the Academy of Natural Sciences in 1896.

Each summer, the Schäffers combed the areas around Glacier, Field, and Banff, collecting new specimens. However, they never ventured far from the railway lines. Charles, by no means a young man, suffered from heart disease and was unable to do anything too strenuous. This was fine with his wife, who also suffered from poor health on occasion. Since childhood, Mary had experienced periodic bouts of neuralgia, which resulted in intense, intermittent pain along a nerve and could be terribly debilitating at times. As a result, Mary considered herself somewhat of a delicate woman and was pleased to limit her mountain adventures to walks near the railway and cosy hotels. For years, neither Schäffer had the slightest urge to camp in the wilderness, climb a mountain, or even go for a trail ride.

Poor health wasn't the only reason Mary had for shying away from mountain adventures. She was also scared. Harbouring a terrible fear of the unknown wilderness, the thought of delving deep into the mountains was nothing if not uncomfortable. Instead of imagining the joys of conquering a peak or fording a river, Mary pictured herself slipping down a mountain or being mauled by a grizzly bear. Her vivid imagination often seemed to get the best of her.

Despite all this, in the summer of 1893, the Schäffers took the plunge and went on a camping trip with friends from Philadelphia. The plan was to spend one night on the shores of Lake Louise, and the idea of sleeping beside the breathtaking lake was exciting even to Mary. Charles approached Tom Wilson, a well-known pioneer outfitter and guide, to prepare the group for the trip. Wilson was happy to help the small party and arranged to have two Stoney guides, William and Joshua Twin, escort the group to Lake Louise and set up camp.

When the day of the trip arrived, the Schäffers and seven friends gathered at Glacier House and waited for a train to take them to Laggan, now the town of Lake Louise. Caught up in the excitement of their upcoming excursion, the inexperienced group agreed it would be fun to travel the 60 kilometres on top of a boxcar. Though Mary later wondered who'd come up with this bizarre idea, at the time she was keen to ride with the others. Her only misgivings arose when she saw the tiny ladder she had to climb to get to the roof. But not wanting to miss out on the new experience, she crept up the ladder and tried to make herself comfortable. After many delays, the train set out with nine eager easterners perched on its rooftop. While the lofty trip was unique, the beautiful mountain views were somewhat marred by the engine soot that showered the passengers.

Upon arriving at Laggan Station, the blackened group was met by William and Joshua Twin, their wives and children, and a selection of horses. Mary, who once would have gawked at the Native peoples before her, gawked instead at the horses — since childhood, she'd held a profound fear and distrust of horses. As her anxiety mounted, Mary approached William and offered him a bribe. Putting 50¢ in his hand, she asked him to point out which horse would get her to Lake Louise safely. When her best bet was pointed out, Mary felt even worse. William had pointed to the homeliest pony of the group. But Mary, trusting her guide, and her 50¢, awkwardly mounted the horse and hoped for the best.

Mary Schäffer

Within moments, the travellers were starting the next leg of their great adventure. At first Mary was terrified of her horse, certain that he would buck her off or charge ahead of the others. But, as William had promised, the modest pony turned out to be the best of the bunch. Just as Mary was beginning to feel at ease, just as she began to entertain the possibility of more riding adventures, the 5 kilometre trip was over. Mary was embarrassed when she realized that the Twins and their families had come all the way from Morley, a distance of more than 125 kilometres, just to travel 5 kilometres with a bunch of tourists. Nonetheless, the group was in great spirits, feeling, as Mary described, that they had just "done something."

However, Mary's enthusiasm dissipated as soon as it came time to camp. The lakeshore was dismally uncomfortable to a woman accustomed to fancy hotel rooms. Mosquitoes bothered Mary and the others all evening, and the romance of sleeping beneath the stars was quickly forgotten. Exhausted from her eventful day, Mary skipped her first campfire supper and headed for the closest tent. There, she caught a terrible chill and took cover under a myriad of blankets, all of which, to her disgust, reeked of horse. Sneezing and shivering uncontrollably, she grew certain that she was suffering from typhoid fever and resigned herself to the possibility of freezing to death.

Mary's self-pity was interrupted by one of her friends. Suspecting she was cold, this friend had taken a hot stove lid into the tent to help warm her. Unfortunately, as the friend approached Mary's mattress, she tripped and the hot lid banged Mary in the head. Instead of crying, Mary began to laugh uncontrollably. Once the laughter subsided, the hot lid was placed between the two women, and both fell asleep. Waking up the next morning, teeth chattering and body aching, Mary promised herself she would never camp in the Canadian Rockies again.

Chapter 3

Getting Brave

For several summers after the Lake Louise experience, Mary kept her vow to never again camp in the Rockies. She was happy to dwell in the luxury of Glacier House, and she cheerfully continued to help Charles with his botanical work, developing her artistic and photographic skills in the process. When she wasn't working with Charles, Mary liked to read in the hotel's sitting room, where she devoured book after book about the nature and history of the Rockies. With every new tidbit of information, Mary grew more enamoured with the area.

The Schäffers became regular summer fixtures at Glacier House and, as a result, were around for many exciting events. Mountaineers and explorers were conquering peaks and delving into new lands all around them. Mary listened eagerly as tales of these adventurers' exploits were recounted at Glacier House. She also read anything she could about the adventurers, impressed by their bravery — and somewhat envious of their abilities.

With every book she read and every gripping tale she was told, Mary became more open to the possibility of venturing deeper into the mountains. She wanted to see for herself the beauty of the untouched wilderness. For the first time in years, she also wanted to feel the rush of adventure, much like she had when she was younger. She even considered camping again.

In the summer of 1898, Mary could wait no longer. Though apprehensive, she was ready to embark on a new, albeit tame, mountain adventure. At the beginning of the season, she and Charles accompanied members of the Philadelphia Photographic Society from Philadelphia to British Columbia. The group then took a private railway car to Field, where their guides were waiting. Again, Mary was confronted with her fear of horses, as the plan was to travel on horseback through the Yoho Valley to Emerald Lake. However, she squelched her fear, and the excursion was a success — the group became the first tourists to trek through the Yoho Valley.

Invigorated from this journey, Mary and Charles later pushed on to Revelstoke. They checked into what Mary described as "the little red-brown CPR hotel" and were immediately awed by the inn's view of the Columbia Valley. However, after drinking in the view and enjoying a good meal or two, the Schäffers came to a wary realization: "There was very little for idlers like ourselves to 'do' at that time, no nice nearby trips and but one 'sight.'"

The "sight" was the canyon at the Big Bend of the Columbia River. To view it, Mary and Charles would have to travel well beyond the railway stations they were usually so careful to border. But since it seemed there was nothing else to do, the Schäffers decided to venture into the wilderness and hired a driver to take them the 8 kilometres from Revelstoke to the Big Bend in a horse-drawn wagon. Relieved that she did not have to ride the horses pulling the vehicle, Mary sat back and enjoyed the scenery. After 5 kilometres had been traversed, the driver stopped at the canyon of the Big Bend, informing the couple that the point of interest must be reached by foot. Wary about hiking, Mary and Charles stumbled out of the wagon and watched as their means of transportation was securely tied to a tree.

Then the Schäffers started their first real wilderness adventure. For two people unaccustomed to roughing it, the hike was somewhat treacherous and certainly daring. Following a narrow path between the high canyon walls and the rushing Columbia rapids below, Mary could not help but think of the many gold seekers and explorers who had drowned in the raging river. She also thought of the adventurers who had followed the path she now travelled and wondered where they were, and if they'd taken the time to notice the beauty that had surrounded them. The hike to Big Bend had a profound effect on Mary. In her later years, she looked back on it and recorded, "It was my first baptism in the sadness and the wildness and the beauty of the Canadian Alps. I had lived hitherto always within the sound of the shrieking engines and passing trains of the mountain division, and the impression made, was one to last always."

As Mary and Charles breathlessly took in their surroundings, they noticed that daylight was beginning to fade. It was time to turn back. But upon their return, they discovered that the wagon and horses were gone, finding only a perfectly turned wheel track that presumably led all the way back to Revelstoke. Fuming that they had to walk another 5 kilometres to town, the Schäffers tried to figure out why they had been left behind. As it turned out, the horses had been removed as a practical joke pulled on the driver by his friends. Knowing this did not appease the Schäffers' irritation, an irritation that intensified when the driver insisted on being paid.

Despite the poor end to the Big Bend journey, Mary was not discouraged from embarking on other mountain exploits. After their short visit to Revelstoke, she and Charles spent the rest of that summer at Glacier House. Though they were back among familiar surroundings, something had changed. Mary was no longer happy simply collecting specimens by the railway tracks. Her trips in the Yoho and Columbia Valleys had whetted her appetite for more sight-seeing — sightseeing beyond the train's ever-present whistle.

Mary figured that the best way to explore the wilderness would be to join Mary Vaux and her family in their mountain expeditions. Like the Schäffers, the Vauxes had been regular summer fixtures at Glacier House. Beginning in 1894, Mary Vaux and her brothers, George and William, had undertaken an annual measurement of both the Illecillewaet and Asulkan Glaciers. The family's scientific exploits and enthusiasm for the mountains also took them on countless hikes and climbs. Mary's friendship with the Vauxes made her feel comfortable enough to accompany them on at least a few of their excursions.

The first was a hike to Bear Creek Falls in the summer of 1898. Much of this journey was through uncut brush, making it exasperating for the inexperienced Mary. But she prevailed and, upon reaching the destination, felt exhilarated. In fact, the delicate Mrs. Schäffer felt so great that she walked back to Glacier House at the end of the day, rather than taking the train, as planned.

Mary got such joy from the hike to Bear Creek Falls that she was ready to embark on an even bigger adventure. Though frightened at the thought of mountaineering, she agreed to join the Vauxes on a climbing expedition. On August 28, she accompanied the family on their ascent of Mount Abbott. Though it is unclear whether she attained the summit, she was successful enough in her own mind to join the Vauxes on other expeditions in the remaining weeks of that summer and in summers to come.

Although Mary was beginning to explore the wilderness she had once been happy to avoid, she still harboured fears. She was still frightened by the unpredictability of horses, still nervous about the sudden appearance of a grizzly bear, and still uncomfortable with mountaineering. But she was getting braver, and while her mountain adventures were relatively tame, they made her feel good about herself. Of course, it was also great to return to the comfort of a warm hotel room and a supportive husband at the end of the day.

The whole time, Mary continued collecting, photographing, and painting plant specimens. Every fall, upon returning to Philadelphia, she kept her mind on the Rockies by working diligently on her paintings and lantern slides. In between attending scores of social and family functions, she happily planned small mountain excursions for the summers to come. At times, Mary's health problems overpowered her enthusiasm. Her neuralgia acted up on several occasions, some bouts more debilitating than others. In the spring of 1903, she was so weak that Charles doubted they would make it west that year. But his wife's growing devotion to the great outdoors won out, and the Schäffers made it to the Rockies for a short, albeit significant, holiday.

In July of that year, a chance encounter at Glacier House inspired Mary's sense of adventure more than any book she had read or story she had heard. One afternoon, while relaxing in the hotel's office, she watched as an older man conversed with the woman behind the check-in desk. Straining to hear what the man was saying, Mary made out the words "Palliser" and "Kicking Horse" and realized that the stranger was talking about the 1857 Palliser Expedition. Her excitement began to grow. In 1857, Captain John Palliser led an expedition team of scientists across Canada's southern prairies and through the Rocky Mountains. The goal of the expedition was to collect much-needed information about many unknown areas, including the plains south of the North Saskatchewan River and the southern passes through the Rockies. While exploring, the team would also map each region's geographic features. Along with Palliser, the men on the expedition included botanist Eugène Bourgeau, secretary and astronomer John W. Sullivan, magnetical observer Lt. Thomas W. Blakiston, and geologist and naturalist Dr. James Hector. The reports and maps put together by these men opened doors to settlement in the future province of Alberta. They were also incredibly helpful to railway planners who wanted to build through the mountains.

Mary had read all about the Palliser Expedition and wanted to hear more of what the man had to say. She rose from her chair and, as politely as possible, budded in to the conversation, asking demurely if she could listen. The woman behind the desk, familiar with Mary's curiosity, smiled knowingly and introduced the stranger as Sir James

Hector. Mary could not believe her luck. Standing before her was the last-known living explorer of Palliser's day, a man of huge celebrity and accomplishment. As she listened attentively, Sir James described many of his misadventures. He explained the expedition's difficulty in gaining access into the mountains due to a group of distrusting Native peoples. He then described how he gained their trust by providing them with much-needed medical care. After a while, the expedition members were even offered native guides to lead them over the mountainous terrain. Finally, Sir James relayed an incident in which he was kicked by his horse and knocked unconscious next to a rushing river somewhere near Field. Thinking their companion was dead, the other members of the team dug a grave, but just as they were about to toss him in, Sir James awoke. Upon regaining his equilibrium, he named the river Kicking Horse.

This was the first time since 1861 that Sir James had been back to the Canadian Rockies, and he planned to visit Golden, as well as the river he had so appropriately named. But for that night, he was happy to sit with the Schäffers at Glacier House, entertaining them with more of his mountain adventures. Mary was invigorated by his stories, feeling more empowered to push her own fears of misadventure aside.

But Sir James never made it to Field or the Kicking Horse River. The next morning, his son grew ill, and Charles diagnosed him with advanced appendicitis, insisting that he be rushed to the nearest hospital, in Revelstoke. But his condition was too far advanced, and only two days after the diagnosis, Douglas Hector died. Too broken-hearted to continue his journey, Sir James went home, never to return to North America. While Mary was saddened by the sudden death of the young man, her brief meeting with Sir James had left her stimulated. Although still weak from her recent bout of neuralgia and forced to put off plans for any mountain exploits that summer, Mary was stirred by thoughts of adventures to come.

This anticipation was quickly smothered upon returning to Philadelphia in the fall. In November 1903, Dr. Charles Schäffer passed away of an apparent heart attack. Mary was heartbroken, her grief compounded by the fact that her mother had died only a couple of months earlier, and her father died less than a month after Charles. Her main sources of love and support were gone, and Mary felt terribly alone and vulnerable. These feelings intensified when she learned that she was left with very little money. Incessant charity, sad impracticality, and substantial losses in the stock market had depleted both Charles's and her parents' fortunes. At 42 years old, Mary Schäffer was widowed, orphaned, and nearly broke. Her untroubled days of mountain views in the summer and city life in the winter now seemed like a distant memory.

Chapter 4

Starting Over

Until the fall of 1903, Mary had lived a life of leisure. From her sheltered childhood to her comfortable marriage, she always had someone to rely on, someone willing to give her anything she wanted. But with the deaths of Charles and her parents, she could no longer enjoy this carefree dependence. Mary now had to learn — quickly — how to make meagre ends meet. And she had to do it alone.

Although in a state of shock and sadness, Mary knew that she could not sit around lamenting her situation. She could not afford to — dwindling savings meant that she had to recoup Charles's monetary losses or face bankruptcy.

Suddenly devoid of her support systems, and realizing they hadn't been so reliable after all, Mary learned "the bitter lesson, to count [her] pennies, to lean on no one and make the best of crumbling fortunes."

While she had many wealthy friends and acquaintances in Philadelphia, Mary chose not to let them know about her predicament. Out of pride, and a great respect for her deceased loved ones, she tried not to let on that much of the money that had supported her affluent lifestyle was gone. Instead, she set out to regain those funds as quickly as possible. For help in doing so, Mary turned to an influential friend she had made in the Canadian Rockies — Richard B. Bennett.

Based in Calgary, Alberta, R. B. Bennett was a prominent lawyer and a member of the Legislative Assembly of the North-West Territories who later became the prime minister of Canada. While living in Calgary, Bennett became keenly interested in the nearby mountains and made numerous visits to Banff and surrounding areas. Consequently, he became friendly with the Schäffers. Remembering that Bennett had a great deal of financial savvy, and appreciating that he was far removed from the prying eyes of Philadelphia society, Mary wrote to him asking for advice. Luckily, Bennett's advice paid off quickly. Mary put much of her declining fortune toward investments that he recommended, and many were soon paying excellent dividends. Within a year, she had regained enough money to remain financially secure for the rest of her life.

Starting Over

But financial security was not enough to heal Mary's heart, and she was still terribly lonely. She found some comfort in the family she had left, but their customary requests for loans and donations often left her feeling frustrated and abused. She also felt somewhat hurt by her circle of Philadelphia friends and acquaintances. Never having a great deal of interest in city trends and the latest fashions to begin with, Mary lost any cares she had about dressing in current styles. As a result, she was ignored by many of the people she had known for years, "banned from parties because [her] clothes were not correct."

The winter of 1904 was a dismal one for Mary Schäffer. Widowed after 14 years of marriage, with no parents to give comfort and few friends to provide distraction, she was suffering through a difficult time. But common sense and remarkable reserves of inner strength forced Mary to realize that in order to heal, she had to act. She needed a project. A distraction.

Mary decided that her most meaningful distraction would be to complete the guide to the Canadian Rockies flora that she and Charles had always planned to write. This enormous project would allow her to escape to the mountains, while still honouring her beloved husband and the important work he had begun. It was the perfect challenge for the grieving Mary, but it would not be an easy one. For starters, Mary's knowledge of botany was rudimentary. Like most wives of the day, she had been a faithful helper to her husband but had learned very little of his craft. She had been happy to press, paint, and photograph specimens, leaving the scientific identification and classification to Charles. Mary knew full well that the scientific community might not approve of her decision to forge ahead with the botanical guide, but she didn't let this stop her. As she later wrote, "To know your terrible ignorance is a great handicap, but I had reached the point where I knew I must lay down the playing with botany and take it up in seriousness for I had touched the place where there was no longer the companion to help me in my work and I knew I must face the future alone."

Mary may have been facing the future alone, but she needed a partner — a real scientist — to help her complete the botanical guide. Wanting someone she trusted and respected, Mary turned to Stewardson Brown, curator of the herbarium of the Academy of Natural Sciences in Philadelphia and an esteemed botanist who had worked with Charles. Aware that getting Brown to help with the project might be difficult, Mary promised him full credit for the book. Working from Philadelphia, he would analyze the specimens that Mary and Charles had already collected, as well as new specimens she planned to gather in the coming summers. Once collection and analysis were complete, Brown would carry on with the actual writing. Brown readily agreed to the proposal, pleased to help complete his colleague's work, and happy to take the credit.

Content with her deal with Brown, Mary now faced other

obstacles. She and Charles had collected all kinds of botanical specimens, but they had never ventured deep into the mountains. In order for a botanical study of the Canadian Rockies to be complete, Mary knew she would have to travel farther than she and Charles had cared to go. To do this, she would have to learn the skills of a true mountain enthusiast. She would also have to overcome her fear and distrust of horses.

To help, Mary turned to friend and outfitter Tom Wilson. Wilson had been responsible for outfitting the Schäffers on their 1893 camping trip to Lake Louise. In subsequent years, he had also taken Mary on small hikes and excursions, dragging "a poor little delicate tourist to points she would not have reached." By 1904, Wilson had accrued several competent guides for his outfitting business. Mary asked him to suggest someone who could toughen her up and train her for the long trail adventures that lay ahead. Wilson assigned her to the care of Billy Warren, a young guide who had arrived in Banff two years earlier.

Born in Essex County, England, in 1880, Billy Warren had studied accounting before enlisting in the Imperial Yeomanry and serving in the Boer War. Unhappy with his post-war job as a clerk in London, he moved to Canada, where he envisioned brighter prospects. But Billy had a hard time finding employment in his new home. Countless Englishmen were emigrating to Canada at that time, and soon prospective employers in Canadian cities were putting up signs that read "No Englishmen Need Apply." After seeing one too many of these signs, Billy decided to test his luck in Banff. He arrived in the humble mountain community in 1902, 22 years old and very eager. Tom Wilson immediately saw the young man's potential and hired him as a packer.

By 1904, Billy had demonstrated that he was a skilled guide, as well as a kind and patient teacher. Wilson was certain he was the perfect leader to suit Mary's temperament — and he was right. Mary liked Billy almost immediately and later wrote of him, "There are older ones, there are better hunters perhaps, with wider experience in forest lore, more knowledge of the country, but for kindness, good nature (such a necessary adjunct), good judgment under unexpected stress, he had no superior."

With a guide and a botanist lined up, Mary had one more issue to resolve before diving into her work. At the turn of the 20th century, it was frowned upon for women to travel with men who were not their husbands or relatives. Although Mary generally cared little about society rules, she cared enough about her own reputation to seek out a few women to bring along on her mountain adventures. After some searching for women who shared her interest in mountain flora and who could travel in the summer, Mary recruited three single teachers from Philadelphia: Miss Day, Miss Farr, and Miss James. Soon, Mary and her companions were travelling to the Canadian Rockies, excited to begin collecting new specimens.

The summer of 1904 was a busy one. Under the guidance of Billy Warren, Mary and her companions made frequent forays to the Yoho and Ptarmigan Valleys, both of which were rich in botanical specimens. They spent more than four months gathering new flora for the guidebook, all the while learning how to handle their horses on difficult terrain. Slowly, Mary was overcoming her fear of horses, realizing that the animals were not the unruly beasts she once thought.

Overcoming this fear was as much a matter of pride as it was necessity. Wanting to appear competent, Mary worked hard not to let her anxiety or ignorance show to her guide or her companions: "I was forced to sit with beating heart as a tiny atom of horse-flesh made his way up some impossible looking place, to learn to balance myself as my live vehicle took an unexpected leap over some soft place where a treacherous stream might have sunk us both in mire, to attempt to look wise in horse lore before the critic who was ever with me on these botanical hunts and to absorb with sickening knowledge the fact that he knew I was a 'tenderfoot' of the worst type when he would casually tell me the manner in which I held my feet in the stirrups was not at all right."

Mary never lost her impulse to hide her fear when facing a treacherous incline or raging river, but after a while, her need to appear skilled on a horse seemed to disappear. While returning from an excursion in the Ptarmigan Valley that summer, she was calmly riding down a mountain, confident that her horse, Eva, would get her to the bottom safely. As she took in the sights, Mary suddenly felt herself slipping awfully close to Eva's ears. Realizing that something was amiss, she began to call out to Billy, but she was too late. Before she knew it, she had fallen over Eva's head, her left foot caught in the stirrup. Dangling precariously between ground and horse, Mary looked at her shocked companions, then at Eva, who had been brought to her knees. Instead of hiding her face in embarrassment or crying out in pain, Mary began to howl with laughter. Her foot still caught in the stirrup, her horse still on its knees, she laughed and laughed until a flustered Billy Warren managed to free her.

Mary's horse skills improved with each outing, and by the end of that summer, her confidence had grown. She and her companions gathered more than 40 new specimens for the project. Even better, her adventurous spirit, which had been soaring the summer before, had returned. After a year of tragedies and bitter blows, Mary was once more on her way to becoming the mountain adventurer she so deeply longed to be.

Chapter 5
Yahe-Weha

ary's decision to complete the botanical guide to the Canadian Rockies was one of the best she could have made. She dedicated herself to the work, collecting specimens, drying them, then photographing and painting them. The project was huge, and Mary threw herself into it. In the process, she discovered her independence, and her lonely heart began to heal. She described her hard work as "a great panacea for broken threads in life," and whenever she found a new type of flower, she experienced "a glow which helped life's path immeasurably."

On occasion, Mary's zeal led to near catastrophes. Once, while attempting to gather some flowers below the

Mary Schäffer

Banff Springs Hotel, Mary came close to contracting a contagious disease. Remembering that several summers earlier she had seen a bed of gentians in the area, she marched along the banks of the Spray River toward where they had been, eager to add them to her collection. As she plodded along, she heard a yell and looked up to see a man waving his arms madly. He was motioning her to turn away. Indignant that a man would have the gall to keep her away from her flowers, Mary ignored his gestures and kept walking. The man continued to wave his arms, and Mary continued to disregard him. Growing angry, she arrogantly reasoned that she had known the area long before he had, and if anyone was to leave, it would have to be him. She wanted her flowers! The two opponents scrambled over logs and through bushes, drawing nearer to each other. Finally, Mary heard the man's voice over the rushing river, yelling with frightening clarity, "You'd better go back! There's a smallpox camp here!"

Thoroughly embarrassed, Mary turned around and walked away with what little poise she had left. But she could not forget those gentians. Two weeks after the incident, she heard that the smallpox camp had dispersed and all the contaminated materials had been burned. Determined to collect the elusive blue flowers, Mary and her companions headed for the abandoned site, holding their skirts tight around their legs. When they reached the camp, they discovered that there were no gentians at all. Fortunately, the hike was not a complete waste. Before leaving, the women noticed a perfect

48

bush of trumpet honeysuckle. The flowers reminded Mary of her grandmother's garden in Philadelphia, and she knew that they would be an important addition to the guidebook. Ignoring the fact that they were taking specimens from a site that had recently been bombarded by pestilence, the women gathered the flowers and left the camp. For several days, they watched for signs of smallpox. When none arose, they "concluded that nature was an excellent disinfectant."

While the summer of 1904 had seen Mary grow increasingly comfortable in the wilderness, the next summer was marked with one new adventure after another. In 1905, Mary and her companions ventured beyond the Ptarmigan and Yoho Valleys into the country bordering the North Saskatchewan River. Guided again by Billy Warren, the group made several trips to the area, collecting a variety of flora. The pack trips became increasingly longer, the terrain more challenging, but Mary, who was starting to love horses, was turning into a seasoned mountain enthusiast. She was even beginning to like camping.

Returning to Glacier House after one trek, Mary was invited to embark on her most exciting adventure yet. Charles Deutschman, a former prospector and hunter, asked her if she would like a personal tour of Deutschman's Caves. Just a year earlier, as he was exploring the Cougar Brook Valley, Deutschman had discovered a series of caves beneath the brook. With only a tallow candle to light his way, he investigated the strange system of caverns, which are now known as the Nakimu Caves. He realized that the caves would attract the more adventurous tourists at Glacier House and developed wooden walkways and ladders to facilitate access. Although Deutschman had already taken several men to see "his" caves, no women had yet entered them. Of course, this was about to change. Both Mary Schäffer and Mary Vaux readily agreed to do the honour.

On July 31, 1905, the two Marys set out for their latest exploit. Accompanied by Deutschman and his Swiss guide, Edward Freuz, they began the daylong journey to Cougar Valley. Mary Schäffer was delighted when she discovered that the valley was full of rare flora to add to her ever-growing collection. After a long day of travel and a successful round of plant gathering, the foursome retired to tents for the night.

The next day, the women were awakened at four o'clock, and after a hearty breakfast they were led to the caves. With ropes around their waists, they were lowered down the face of a cliff until they came to a gaping hole through which they had to crawl. Upon entering the caves, Mary Schäffer and Mary Vaux descended a ladder into a chamber called the Auditorium. Lighting their way with large candles, they took in the sights of the vaulted gallery. The candlelight showed a stream of blood-red water as it rushed by them and tumbled over a steep cliff. From the Auditorium, the women were guided through a series of holes, each decreasing in size until they had to literally squeeze themselves through.

Yahe-Weha

The last hole they saw that day was the most frightening for Mary Schäffer. Called Big Hole, this cavity was so deep that the end of it could not be distinguished. As she fought to see in the darkness, Mary heard Deutschman order her to lean back against the rock. She followed his orders and felt an ice-cold trickle of water moisten her neck. Thinking she was standing on a sturdy ledge, Mary was shocked when a flash of Deutschman's pocket light revealed that she and her guide were standing together on a tiny outcropping that protruded over a "sheer abyss of eighty feet with a river thundering below." Realizing she was actually standing on Deutschman's feet, and that his sole source of support was the rope tied around her waist, Mary had finally had enough adventure for the day. She turned her head ever so slightly and said weakly, "Let's get out; this is rather getting on my nerves." Deutschman complied and they were shortly climbing the steep incline to the cave entrance. Happy to see sunlight again, Mary breathed a sigh of relief once everyone emerged alive.

Despite this unnerving incident, Mary enjoyed her tour of Deutschman's Caves. She had come through the excursion unscathed and, in the process, collected some valuable plants. Prompted by these successes, she decided to give mountaineering another try soon after returning from Cougar Brook Valley.

But Mary soon realized that climbing was not a sport she wished to pursue. As she followed her guide and companions up Mount Wilcox, she was barely able to enjoy the good company or the beautiful scenery. Instead, she spent much of the climb "with head held high, teeth bitten into lips and a vow in [her] heart to look at things from a lower level." While Mary was happy to see the spectacular panoramas that could only be viewed from the mountaintop, she was even more delighted when she reached the mountain's base. When the climb was over, Mary resolved that mountaineering was definitely not for her: "Why do something with your heart in your mouth all the time?"

Although climbing did not appeal to her, Mary continued to thrive in her treasured mountain settings. She loved the pack trips that Billy Warren so dutifully led, and she was growing increasingly brave when it came to camping. One of the most exciting early camping expeditions she planned took place in the summer of 1906 — a 17-day pack trip to the Kootenay Plains on the North Saskatchewan River. At first, Mary meant to bring only one companion, but as they talked excitedly about their journey, a "quiet, little eastern woman" asked if she and another woman could join them. Believing that the more campers there were the merrier, Mary readily consented to the stranger's request. Soon after, yet another woman asked to come along. By the time the day of departure arrived, five women, outfitted by Billy Warren and Bob Campbell, set out for their two-week adventure. Among them were Mary, Henrietta Tuzo, Dorothea Sharp, and Zephine Humphrey. The quiet little eastern woman was Mary Adams, a geology professor from New York whom everyone called Mollie.

Yahe-Weha

It was on this camping trip that Mary learned that more did not mean merrier. Only three days into the excursion, the women had separated "as oil and water." Mary and Mollie discovered that they shared many interests and became fast friends. Their mutual enthusiasm for the journey at hand united them, and they happily shared a tent. The other three women, less enthusiastic and more inclined to complaining, shared another tent. One morning, when the guides began to pound a pan announcing breakfast, Mary and Mollie emerged from their tent and sat down to eat. The others, however, stayed in their tent, giggling and gossiping and holding up the entire day. This was the beginning of a silent friction between the newly devised parties. Mary and Mollie enjoyed every moment of their journey along the North Saskatchewan, but the other women made it clear that they found trail life to be a terrible bore. They felt that Mary was uptight and overbearing, while Mary felt they were being childish.

Despite these disagreements, Mary managed to have a good time. The guides took the group through breathtaking scenery, following the Pipestone Pass and the Siffleur River to the Kootenay Plains. Pleased with the sights, Mary was able to ignore the complaints and sighs of three of her trail mates for most of the trip. But when she discovered that one of them intended to cut the trip short by three days because she longed for a bath, Mary's patience ran out. She was irate that this woman had the gall to ruin a trip she'd been planning for a year, "all for the sake of a bath-tub." She and Mollie began to plot ways in which they could prevent the woman from following through on her designs. Finally, Mary came up with a plan.

The next morning, the camper who "longed the most for the flesh-pots of civilization" announced that they would all be travelling home the following day. Mary, stood up and bravely informed her companion that travelling home the next day would be impossible. In a stern voice she explained, "Tomorrow is Sunday and I never travel on Sundays." This was a bald-faced lie — Mary had always thought Sunday was one of the best days to travel. However, using her religious background as an excuse paid off, and Mary and Mollie restored their journey to its full length.

Once back in the comfort of Glacier House, Mary swore never to camp with a large group of women again. She was willing, though, to travel a great deal more with Mollie Adams. They had forged a powerful friendship, and over the next several years remained steadfast travelling companions, journeying to destinations near and far without a "riffle of disagreement."

Later that summer, Mary and Mollie made another trip to the North Saskatchewan River, following much the same route they had taken with the larger group. Once again, Billy Warren was their chief guide. After a visit to the Kootenay Plains, as well as a side trip to Glacier Lake, they ventured into new territory, travelling over Pinto Pass to Pinto Lake and down the Cline River. On their way back to Laggan, the women decided to make another stop at the Kootenay Plains. Upon their arrival, they dug out their cameras and visited the nearby native camp, where several Stoney families were living. Mary had called on the Stoneys before; in fact, she was becoming a repeat visitor. This time, she met and photographed several people, including members of the Beaver family. She took countless photographs of this gracious group, then presented the daughter, Frances Louise Beaver, with a doll she had made of an "old table napkin stuffed with newspaper." Mary valued the time she spent on the Kootenay Plains with the Stoneys. Their culture fascinated her, and she revelled in the fact that she could finally learn first-hand the traditions and beliefs of a plains people.

The people of the Stoney camp were just as fascinated by Mary. It was not often that a foreigner, let alone a woman, visited their camp, and yet in one season Mary had returned to them on several occasions. Her enthusiasm for their way of life and for the surrounding wilderness led them to call her Yahe-Weha, or Mountain Woman. This was a tremendous honour for someone who, not so long ago, had shuddered at the thought of horses, camping, and places unknown.

In 1906, the guidebook to which Mary Schäffer and Stewardson Brown devoted almost three years of their lives was finally finished. One year later, G. P. Putnam's Sons published *Alpine Flora of the Canadian Rocky Mountains*, by Stewardson Brown. It featured 30 full-page coloured plates and 98 other images, all made from Mary's photographs and watercolour paintings. The book was dedicated to the memory of Charles Schäffer, "who was among the pioneer botanists of the Canadian Rockies, and who early recognized the region as a new and interesting field for study."

Mary had done it. She had overseen the project she and Charles had dreamed of completing. More importantly, she had overcome her grief, her loneliness, and her deeply held fear of the world beyond comfortable hotels and the whistle of a train. She had found peace.

Chapter 6

The Plan

he completion of the botanical guide did not mark an end to Mary's wanderings. If anything, it spurred her on. Having reached her goal, Mary realized that she was thoroughly capable when it came to camping and riding in the mountains. In fact, she had grown to love these activities so much that the idea of demurely retiring to the comfort of upper-middle class Philadelphia society was downright distasteful. Mary was more devoted to the mountains than ever before, and her craving for adventure escalated with each passing day.

For years, Mary had listened in rapture while hunters, trappers, and explorers recounted their thrilling exploits through unmapped terrain. As these mountain men described the beauty of unnamed peaks and valleys, of breathtaking waters and peaceful wildlife, Mary grew anxious to explore the lands deep within the Canadian Rockies. Although she and Mollie Adams had made several journeys to the North Saskatchewan, as well as to the Yoho and Ptarmigan Valleys, all these trips had been relatively short and accessible. Moreover, tourists were rapidly overrunning the easily reached mountain sites. Litter was beginning to mark many trails and campgrounds, upsetting those who sought to preserve the solitude and purity of the wilderness. Mary and Mollie longed to explore beyond those well-travelled areas, to disappear for months into untouched wild regions.

But women did not do that kind of thing back then. In 1906, the trails and backwoods of the Canadian Rockies were considered men's domain. Women could take small trips into the mountains, but they were to leave the exploring and the long months away to the "stronger" sex. Women who showed an interest in wilderness travel were often inundated with "reasons" for avoiding the great outdoors. Women were meant to be demure and refined, and it was frequently argued that life on the trail would be too hard for them. The media perpetuated this idea. Even the *New York Times* insisted that "The ordinary woman travels much better in a Pullman than with a pack train, and is much more efficient in parlor adventures than on long hard trails; for a trail appears more flowery and poetic in print and picture than in reality."

Besides, it was generally assumed that most upper-middle class women were more content shopping, attending tea parties, or managing their maids.

Of course, Mary was no average upper-middle class woman, and frivolous activities held little interest for her. Her Quaker upbringing had stressed the equality of the sexes, and she grew increasingly annoyed that society's mores were restricting her from her newest dream. She later described how she and Mollie hated that they had to "sit with folded hands and listen calmly to the stories of the hills [they] so longed to see, the hills which had lured and beckoned [them] for years before this long list of men had ever set foot in the country."

Finally, the two kindred spirits could take no more. It was time to rebel. Both women wanted to journey into the unknown wilderness, and both knew that — contrary to popular belief — they could do it. Sure, they had listened to countless tales of hardship and hunger. Yes, they had heeded endless warnings about treacherous terrain and unforgiving weather. They knew that exploring the wilderness meant facing uncertain dangers, but these two women felt up for the challenge. With their confidence brimming and their stubbornness goading them on, they "looked each other in the eyes and said: 'Why not? We can starve as well as [men]; the muskeg will be no softer for us than for them; the ground will be no harder to sleep upon; the waters no deeper to swim, nor the bath colder if we fall in,' — so — we planned a trip."

What a trip it would be. The women decided they would depart the following summer, June 1907, and spend at least four months exploring the untrodden wilderness of the Canadian Rockies. However, before they could proceed with their plan, they needed to make sure that someone was willing to guide them. Mary turned immediately to Billy Warren, whom she trusted and treasured above any other guide she knew. It was only natural to ask him to lead the adventure, as he was the one who had so patiently taught Mary all her wilderness skills. There was a distinct possibility that Billy would object to taking two women tourists deep into the unknown. After all, he had seen Mary at her greenest. But much to the women's delight, he readily agreed. Mary took his enthusiasm as a compliment, for it meant that he felt she had "worn a considerable amount of the tenderfoot" from her constitution.

Mary and Mollie gave Billy the money to buy and outfit as many horses as they would need. They also asked him to hire a second guide to accompany the small party. Finding this man was a challenge. The second-in-command had to be skilled in a number of areas. He had to be an excellent packer, a good campfire cook, and a dependable woodsman. Perhaps most importantly, he had to possess unending patience and good nature.

Sid Unwin was chosen for the job. Like Billy, Sid was a well-educated Englishman who had served in the Boer War and later worked as a clerk in London. In 1904, he moved to

Banff to seek out a new life, quickly becoming known for his resourcefulness and determination on the trail. A true gentleman, Sid was the perfect choice. He was also as enthusiastic as the rest of the party and gladly helped Billy prepare for their upcoming expedition.

Mary and Mollie were also busying themselves with plans and preparations. They first had to decide which areas they wished to explore. The North Saskatchewan Valley had fascinated the women the previous summer, and both wanted to investigate the area further. Although Mary was perfectly content with the idea of wandering the region with no real destination, her friends and family could not accept this aimlessness. They wanted to know exactly where she was going; without a distinct objective, what was the point? Mary could not relate to this thinking and later wrote, "It seemed strange at first to think we must announce some settled destination, that the very fact of its being a wilderness was not enough."

Nevertheless, in order to provide an answer, Mary and Mollie made their chief objective "to penetrate the head waters of the Saskatchewan and Athabaska rivers." As it turned out, this answer satisfied only a small percentage of Mary's friends and relatives. The majority of her loved ones were not at all appeased. They could not understand why a woman of her stature wanted to spend four months in uncharted, potentially dangerous, and definitely uncomfortable territory. For Mary's part, she could not understand why her city acquaintances were opposed to her journey: "Why must so many cling to the life of our great cities, declaring there only may the heart hunger, the artistic longings, the lore of the beautiful be satisfied, and thus train themselves to believe there is nothing beyond the little horizon they have built themselves?" She wanted to inform them that "there are some secrets you will never learn, there are some joys you will never feel, there are heart thrills you can never experience, till, with your horse you leave the world, your recognized world, and plunge into the vast unknown."

Of course, plunging into the vast unknown took a great deal of forethought. Having chosen their destination, Mary and Mollie now focussed on preparing themselves in other ways, such as packing provisions. They spent much of the winter experimenting with many forms of dried foods, learning the hard way that the makers of these foods often sacrificed taste for convenience. Dried cabbage, for instance, was so smelly that Mary found it nearly impossible to bring it anywhere close to her mouth. She also had qualms about dried milk, dried eggs, and a strongly recommended sweetener called granulose. But having already ordered and received large quantities of these items, the women dutifully packed them away. Along with these goods, they packed more standard camp grub, including flour, coffee, tea, evaporated potatoes, beans, rice, and bacon.

With provisions taken care of, Mary and Mollie picked out appropriate gear and equipment. Wanting to travel as lightly as possible, the women wrestled with what to bring and what to leave behind. Knowing full well that appearance took a back seat to comfort on the trail, Mary packed only the most necessary apparel. She filled a duffel bag with two thick woollen skirts, a short riding skirt, riding breeches, sturdy hobnailed shoes, low rubber-soled canvas shoes, a buckskin jacket, a sweater, and a few hats. As for other gear, the women, braving potential ridicule from their guides, packed two air mattresses and rested easy at the thought of sleeping comfortably after a long day's travel. Although it was bulky, Mary also packed her plant press, as well as cameras and other photographic material. Mollie threw in a geologist's hammer for herself.

After eight months of preparation, their day of departure came on June 1, 1907. Travelling across the continent in a comfortable rail car, Mary and Mollie stopped briefly in Winnipeg to buy two high-end tents made of Egyptian sailcloth. Their trunks had been checked at Montreal and were to be unloaded at Laggan Station, where the party of four would pick them up before departing into the mountains. Everything seemed to be going exactly as planned. Everything, that is, but the weather.

The winter of 1906–07 had been a fierce one in the Canadian Rocky Mountains, and the spring had not been much better. Upon arriving, Mary and Mollie were greeted by cold, snowy weather, and it looked as though their departure would have to be postponed indefinitely. Having waited so long to begin their journey, they figured they could wait awhile longer and headed to Field to sit out the storms. Mary was pleased to see that the guides were as prepared as she and Mollie, and the small group agreed that no matter what the weather had to offer, they would depart no later than June 20. If they left any later, they risked being unable to cross the rising North Saskatchewan River.

While waiting out the days in Field, Mary and Mollie learned that the outfit of horses for their approaching journey was being held in Banff. Curious and excited to see their new "family," they rushed to the town for a look. When they got there, only two of the horses were available for inspection, and neither appeared all that impressive. In fact, one of them was such a homely looking creature that Mary later wrote, "The sight of [him] was enough to kill even the most deep-seated of horse pride." The women soon learned that none of their expedition horses were experienced on the trail. Regardless, Mary had faith that, with the proper guidance, the creatures — beautiful or not — would learn their roles and do the outfit proud.

As June 20 drew near, Mary and Mollie began their last-minute preparations. Two days before the planned departure date, the women made their way to Laggan to pick up their trunks, only to learn that one was missing. Containing bedding, photographic material, clothing, and the treasured air mattresses, it was among the most valuable of the trunks. The women, both plainly upset, were unsympathetically informed by agent after agent that the missing trunk could be anywhere between Montreal and Vancouver. With little time left before they had to leave, Mary knew she must act fast. She was determined that the loss of a piece of luggage — even an important piece — would not put a stop to her journey. Mary and Mollie hastened to Calgary, where they repurchased as many important articles as possible.

As the women waited to board a train back to Laggan, parcels in hand, they decided to inform the railway's baggage-master-in-chief of their troubles. Having experienced the stony indifference of the station agents at Laggan, the women barely expected sympathy from the executive in Calgary. But to their astonishment, the baggage master took immediate action. He sent messages about the missing trunk in every direction and quickly learned that it had definitely passed through Calgary. When the women boarded the westbound train, he boarded it with them and meticulously inspected the baggage department of every little station between Calgary and Laggan.

By the time the train arrived in Lake Louise, the trunk still had not been found. In one last-ditch effort, the baggage master searched Laggan Station and discovered that the wayward trunk had made its way to the Lake Louise Chalet. Despite earlier assurances that the trunk could not possibly have been shipped to the chalet, there it was, in a highly conspicuous spot. The spot was so conspicuous, in fact, that Mary was amazed none of the other station agents had tripped over it in their search. Instead of getting angry at the incompetence of a few, Mary and Mollie chose to be grateful to the sympathetic man who helped to find their precious cargo. His kindness was the perfect send-off.

The return of the trunk was enough to infuse a new sense of energy and excitement into the upcoming expedition. In a short while, all the trunks' contents were distributed upon the backs of the horses. Everything was falling into place, and, a few days later than their desired departure, the four adventurers set their sights north. The journey that Mary was yearning for had finally begun.

Chapter 7

A True Expedition

T he start of the four-month expedition was anything but promising. Having left Laggan at high noon, the travellers were immediately confronted with ominous clouds and biting winds. Fighting the urge to stay put and sit out the weather yet again, the foursome pushed on through the Bow Valley. They had to reach the North Saskatchewan River as soon as possible because the spring thaw would quickly make it impassable. The group also wanted to push on out of concern for the horses. Camping too close to the railway, and the frequent approach of its trains, would have undoubtedly meant the end for many of the beasts. But the going was tough. The horses thrashed about miserably under the unfamiliar weight of their packs. Accustomed to open spaces, the 11 animals clumsily struggled over fallen timber, muskeg, and weather-beaten trails.

By nightfall, the party had still not found an ideal campsite. The wet weather had turned much of the land into a muddy bog, and in the end, the group was forced to set up their tents on a tiny hill surrounded by muskeg. Mud was everywhere — the miserable campers had to cook in it, eat in it, and sleep in it. Trying to stay optimistic after such a dreary start, the companions assured one another that "it might have been worse."

It got worse the next day. Greeted in the morning by pelting hail, the group packed up quickly, only to rush into bigger troubles. Not far from their abandoned camp, they encountered the worst patch of muskeg yet. The horses, untrained and weighed down by the packs, waded helplessly into the bog. Before anyone knew it, one of the strongest animals, Buck, was sinking in the watery marsh, taking with him more than 90 kilograms of bacon and flour. The horse was saved when one of the quick-thinking guides cut its cargo loose. Down went the bacon, the flour, and Buck, but all three floated to the surface and eventually landed on more solid ground. As Mary later wrote of the incident, "The bacon had had its first bath, but never its last."

Over the course of the summer, the horses provided their keepers with countless moments of entertainment, but countless more moments of dread. The hardworking beasts took turns falling into raging rapids, soaking their cargo, and leading peaceful revolts in their quests for feed or easier terrain. But each was resilient, and in time they became quite professional. Mary came to realize that when shown the right amount of patient consideration, the creatures could become reliable — even lovable — companions: "I shall never believe again that a horse lives with traits so bad, that he cannot be broken of them to a large extent by kindness. Certain it was that there were those in our band who at first were enough to try the patience of a saint, and in the end became perfect masters of their art."

Mary's horse, Nibs, was probably the most masterful of the bunch. He was a latecomer to the fold, obtained about a week into the expedition, when the foursome had a chance encounter with Tom Wilson. Wilson, who had first introduced Mary to Billy Warren, was leading a team of 60 horses from Kootenay Pass to Laggan. As Mary watched the large procession go by, she spotted Nibs, the "flower of the band." In no time, the mighty horse was pulled from one team and added to the other. From then on, Nibs and Mary were virtually inseparable on the trail.

Bidding farewell to Tom Wilson, the group continued on toward the North Saskatchewan. For the last few days, the sun had been shining and the weather had been hot. Although they welcomed the warmth, everyone was aware that with each sunny day, the river's level would rise, making it more dangerous to cross. When they finally reached the North Saskatchewan, they saw that their fears were warranted. It was indeed getting higher, and the group was both anxious and hesitant to ford it. Sid went first, taking the most reliable horse. Together, horse and guide slowly waded from one sandbar to another until they were waiting on the river's north shore. The others followed, each making it across without having to swim. For someone who once wished she had "the courage to turn back" every time she and her horse waded into water, Mary's successful crossing of the mighty North Saskatchewan River was an incredible achievement.

However, within a day or so of the crossing, the group learned that the river had risen so high there could be no turning back until later in the season. Mary felt an inkling of panic. She was trapped in the wilderness, and although it was exactly where she wanted to be, the realization that she was so far from civilization made her lonely. But when a swarm of mosquitoes descended on the camp one night, Mary's loneliness was replaced by a resolve to face the bittersweet challenges of trail life.

The planned route for the expedition was fairly straightforward. Once across the North Saskatchewan, the foursome would make their way to the head of the Athabasca River via the Wilcox and Sunwapta Passes. Parts of the route would be long and difficult. In order to make it easier on the burdened pack horses, the group agreed to establish a base camp, choosing Graveyard Camp, named for the animal bones littering its grounds. Situated near the junction of the Nashan (Alexandra) River and the North Saskatchewan, Graveyard Camp was an ideal takeoff point. The men built a cache about 30 kilometres from the camp, then stored much of the outfit's food there. The idea was to spend the rest of the summer taking long side trips from Graveyard Camp, returning only to replenish their food supply.

The first trip from Graveyard Camp was a trek northwest to Fortress Lake. In 1893, explorer A. P. Coleman had located and named the lake while searching for the elusive Mounts Brown and Hooker, which were then thought to be over 4800 metres in elevation. Upon reading Coleman's enthusiastic description of the lake, Mary decided she needed to see it for herself. The foursome followed a breathtaking trail to Wilcox Pass, glimpsing countless major and minor peaks, and even christening a lovely waterfall.

On the morning of the fourth of July, the group was delayed by a surprising and unwelcome snowstorm. After a brief attempt to explore Wilcox Pass, the foursome gave up and spent the rest of the day in camp, happy to be near the warmth of a crackling campfire. They pushed on the next day, only to find that the lingering snow of the summer had turned Wilcox Pass into what Mary described as one of "the longest, spongiest, most tiresome passes [she had] ever travelled." Despite this, she could not help but feel excited, for she was nearing the valley of the Sunwapta River, an area completely new to her. Unfortunately, the trails along the

Sunwapta didn't get much easier. After several long days of difficult travel, the small outfit reached the Athabasca Valley, but Mary and Mollie were distinctly disappointed by what they saw. The Athabasca River itself was much less grand than they had imagined, and the valley was "arid, fire-swept, and generally non-descript as well as hot and fly ridden."

Disappointed but not discouraged, the team followed the Athabasca and Chaba Rivers toward Mount Quincy. Referring to a map she had brought, Mary was certain that Mount Quincy was very close to Fortress Lake. Excitement escalated when everyone realized they were closing in on their destination. All they had to do now was actually find the lake. The hunt began after a tortuous night battling mosquitoes, when the foursome climbed Mount Quincy in the hope of glimpsing the lake from above. Still uncomfortable with mountain climbing, Mary stifled her fear out of a childish desire to be the first of her group to see Fortress Lake. The climb was miserable; the weather was hot, the mosquitoes were swarming, and heavy brush scratched at her face and arms. Despite these obstacles, Mary made it to the mountain's rock bluffs with little help. However, to reach the top, she had to be tossed from one guide to the other, making her feel so unladylike that once again she "wished climbing had never been invented."

Mary's discomfort disappeared when she glimpsed Fortress Lake. As she had hoped, she was the first of the foursome to see the water, and the sight was remarkable, looking

like a "long, pale, blue-green ribbon tossed in dainty abandon among the fir-clad hills." Two days later, the group
reached the lake's shores, but the area was too spongy and
the surrounding forests too thick for further exploration.
Realizing that precious time was passing, and that there were
other areas to investigate, the group recovered from their
frustration and went to explore other parts of the Athabasca
and Chaba River valleys.

During a leisurely day of trailing in the Athabasca Valley,
the foursome spotted a forest fire in their wake. Immediately,
they began to wonder if their outfit had been responsible for
starting the blaze. After all, they were the only people around
for miles — they must have started the fire. Although everyone assured one another that this was surely not possible,
Mary began to feel terribly guilty. The flames continued to
spread, and, waking up the next morning, Mary was sad to see
that the fire was still ravaging the forests opposite their camp.

As the group picked at their breakfasts, watching the fire
in the distance, Mary noticed that another blaze was burning
much closer to home. The morning campfire had ignited one
of the Egyptian sailcloth tents, and the tent was "going up like
a newspaper!" Within seconds, they had trampled the flames
and were left staring at the damaged stock: "one wash-cloth
half destroyed, a handsome silk neckerchief riddled with
holes, sleeve of a sweater gone, handle of a toothbrush
snapped in the scramble, and worst of all, one half of the tent
gone up in smoke."

Not wanting to dwell on their calamitous breakfast, Mary, Mollie, Billy, and Sid packed up camp. Just as they were ready to set off, an unfamiliar horse bell clanged nearby, and out of the woods came three men and five horses. After general niceties were exchanged, it was learned that the men had come up the Athabasca River from its south side and, having got stuck in an overgrown trail, decided to burn their way out. Though unimpressed with these "timber-cruisers," the friends were relieved that the raging flames on the opposite mountainside were not their doing.

Leaving "Burnt Tent Camp" with light hearts, the group set its sights on tracing the Athabasca to its headwaters at the base of Mount Columbia. Mary had been able to see the majestic mountain from their last fiery campsite, and she could not wait to get a closer look. But before taking the whole outfit into unknown territory, Billy and Sid wanted to go ahead and explore the area. This meant that Mary and Mollie would get a rare — and welcome — day alone in camp. The women usually spent such days the same way. Despite strict warnings from Sid not to meddle in the food or waste the laundry soap, they would jump at both food and soap as soon as the men were out of sight, baking and washing to their hearts' content.

But on this particular day, Mary went straight to the task of fixing the charred tent. While Mollie cooked and did the washing, Mary spent the day patching the burnt Egyptian sail-cloth. The result of the women's work was "a fine fruit-cake, a beautiful bannock, and a very peculiarly shaped but rain-proof tent." Proud of her patchwork, Mary ignored the men's good-natured ribbing when they returned to camp. One thought it resembled a chicken coop, while the other thought it looked more like a snowplough. Mary, hands aching and fingers bruised, thought it "was grace and beauty personified."

Mary soon saw something much more beautiful. After three days of travel in the Athabasca Valley, the foursome came upon the base of Mount Columbia. Having journeyed along green slopes and clear trails, past waterfalls and countless peaks, they were treated to the sight of an exquisitely symmetrical mountain draped in glaciers and snow. The companions spent as much time as they could exploring the base, then they retraced their path and looked for a suitable spot to camp. They had been gone for weeks, and the food supply was getting increasingly low — it was time to return to Graveyard Camp.

One morning on their return journey, Mary awoke to see a thick layer of snow on the ground outside her tent. Knowing a snowstorm meant delays, she happily closed her eyes and went back to sleep. Moments later, she was awakened by a distant voice, then a clearing of the throat at her and Mollie's tent door. Shaking off the vestiges of sleep, Mary was surprised to see a stranger, in glasses and gentleman's clothing, standing before her. The man's appearance instantly took her back to the drawing rooms of Philadelphia, and the two strangers exchanged pleasantries despite their less than formal circumstances. The gentleman then asked if there were any men in their camp, and Mary obligingly pointed to the oddly shaped tent just metres away. With a smile and a bow of his head, the stranger headed for the chicken coop, leaving Mary and Mollie to ponder his identity.

When the gentleman left the camp, the women rushed to the guides to get more information. Billy reported that the man was part of another outfit camped 3 kilometres away, and that, having seen the foursome's horses, he sought out their party for a suggested route across Wilcox Pass. The gentleman had left without any clue as to who he was, save the statement that he had "been to Fortress Lake in '93." As the women and their guides ate breakfast, they continued to ponder the stranger's identity. Then someone remembered that 1893 was the year A. P. Coleman had discovered Fortress Lake.

Always a sucker for explorers and strangers, Mary insisted they find the man. As they searched through pelting snow and harsh winds, four men and nine horses came into view. It was the stranger's party. Going straight to the gentleman she had met that morning, Mary bowed her head politely, then asked with forced nonchalance if he had met A. P. Coleman while at Fortress Lake in 1893. The answer was better than she could have dreamed. The gentleman was A. P. Coleman's brother, and Coleman himself was among their party. Mary could not believe it. A. P. Coleman, the man whose writings and advice she had read and heeded throughout the Athabasca Valley, the man "whose name had been on [their] lips for weeks," was right in front of her. Forgetting all sense of propriety, Mary headed for Coleman and proceeded to deluge the explorer with questions about his exploits. After spending much of the snowy morning together, the two outfits parted ways, and Mary and her companions returned to their camp. By the time they said goodbye, Mary was certain the exasperated Coleman brothers must have been glad to see her go.

Inspired by yet more tales of adventure, Mary and the others headed back to Graveyard Camp. Upon their arrival, the men continued on to retrieve more grub from the cache, and the women had another day to themselves. This time, Mary and Mollie spent the day taking photographs in the surrounding wilderness. Not far from camp, they encountered Jimmy Simpson, a well-known guide and trapper, and a good friend. With him was a "charming little English lady" named Mary de la Beach-Nichol, who had hired Simpson to help her collect butterflies. Seeing this London society lady, Mary felt conspicuous. Having now spent two months in the deep of the mountains, there was very little Philadelphia left in her appearance. Clad in riding breeches, a boy's shirt, and a buckskin coat, Mary knew she looked nothing like a society lady. The skirts she'd packed had long been passed over for the more practical breeches and, having escaped the "village and critics" of civilization, she no longer rode sidesaddle.

Despite Mary's discomfort with her own appearance, she and Mollie invited Simpson and "the butterfly lady" to camp nearby. The invitation was readily accepted and, in exchange, the two women were asked to join the newcomers for supper. With Billy and Sid gone for the night, Mary accepted the invitation enthusiastically. In fact, her enthusiasm just embarrassed her more: "The alacrity with which we accepted their invitation to supper that night was a positive disgrace, but we were so tired of mouldy tea, etc., and butter and jam would be such a delicious change that we quite forgot our manners." The women and Jimmy Simpson enjoyed their dinner party and talked around the campfire well into the night.

Billy and Sid returned with food the next day, so Mary and Mollie invited Simpson and Mary de la Beach-Nichol to "their house" for another meal around a blazing campfire. The guests left Graveyard Camp the following morning, and the foursome prepared for their next expedition, this time to view the south face of Mount Columbia and to glimpse the great Columbia Icefield. To reach their destination, they followed the Nashan (Alexandra) River to Thompson Pass. Here they became the first people to cross the pass with pack horses, a distinction that garnered great excitement from the women, who wanted so desperately to break new ground. Travelling through the pass was difficult, as it abounded with fallen trees and narrow rock ledges. But the group pressed on — Mary was set on seeing the plains of ice that had reportedly left earlier explorers awestruck. However, when Mary finally reached her destination, the weather turned so cold that she was glad to cut the sightseeing short and return to camp.

A True Expedition

The last side trip the group took from Graveyard Camp was a September expedition northeast to see Brazeau Lake. While Mary and Mollie were anxious to see this lake, there was another body of water they hoped to reach as well. When the foursome had visited with Jimmy Simpson earlier in the season, he had told them about a secret lake hidden somewhere beyond the Brazeau. Simpson had heard of this lake from Native peoples who had once hunted its shores for beavers. It was known as Chaba Imne, or Beaver Lake. Intrigued by the thought of seeing a lake known to only a few, the group decided they would try to find it. They pushed off on their northeast route, reaching Brazeau Lake via Nigel Pass. After investigating the lake, they grew excited to begin the search for Chaba Imne.

However, the night before the search was to begin, the weather turned ugly. Snow and wind followed rain and thunderstorms, and the party was forced to remain in camp for several days. As soon as the weather cleared, the group began the hunt. For days they tackled treacherous terrain, pushing their horses and fighting against ice and snow. Despite their determined search for Chaba Imne, all they could find were walls of rock and "glacier after glacier." Disappointed, and well aware that their summer was coming to an end, the companions gave up the search and headed one final time to Graveyard Camp.

The return journey through Cataract Pass was a nightmare for Mary. Blinded by the bright sunshine reflecting off the snow, she was forced to wear bandages on her eyes. In pain and sightless, she had to rely on Nibs to follow as close behind Billy as he could. Bombarded by wayward branches and timber, Mary was soon bruised black and blue. To make matters worse, the snow had obliterated any signs of a trail, and in the struggle to find their way, the outfit was delayed by days. Food was getting scarce, and there was a good distance to go before reaching the main cache. The only option was for the men to cross the dangerous Pinto Pass, which would get them to the cache faster. Stopping at Pinto Lake, Billy and Sid set up camp for Mary and Mollie, then left to retrieve the food. By the time they returned, Mary's eyes had recovered sufficiently for her to travel once more.

Slowly, the group made its way down the Cline River. When they reached the Kootenay Plains, the chilly weather disappeared and it was like summer again. Enjoying a few days' rest at their much-loved spot, Mary and Mollie visited with the Stoney band they had got to know the year before. During their final evening on the plains, the foursome attended a makeshift dinner party hosted by an outfitter named Elliot Barnes. Among the guests was Sampson Beaver, a Stoney man whose family Mary had known for two seasons. Still disappointed at not having found Chaba Imne, Mary asked Beaver if he was familiar with the mysterious lake. As it turned out, he had been there once, more than 16 years ago, when just a boy. Mary was aware that Stoneys didn't like to reveal information about their hunting grounds, but she boldly asked Beaver if he would draw her a map to the lake. Beaver requested that he be paid for the information, but Mary would have none of it, reminding him of the many gifts she'd brought to his family. The sheepish Beaver then drew a rough diagram from memory. Pleased with herself, and already planning her next adventure, Mary packed the treasured piece of paper away for safekeeping.

The next day, the companions began their trip back to civilization. It was October, and the months of blissful freedom were coming to an end. In one last effort to extend their journey, the group decided to vary the return route. Instead of taking the familiar Bow Pass, they travelled over Howse Pass, an historic fur trade route of the Hudson's Bay Company. Spurred on by the fact that earlier explorers had found the pass challenging, the outfit eagerly made its way over to the unfamiliar route. At first they found it surprisingly easy to navigate, but once they reached its far side, they inadvertently diverted from the main trail. For the next two days, they struggled up steep inclines and over fields of boulders, trying to find their way back to a trail. The group grew concerned as yet another day was nearing its end and no horse feed — or trail — had been found. As the horses and their keepers grew weaker and more miserable, the ever-reliable Billy discovered plenty of grass in a nearby valley. Within minutes the party had reached the valley, set up camp, and started dinner.

The next morning, Mary and Sid explored a path that took them to the shoulder of an unknown peak. From their

lookout, the two picked out the familiar mountains that surrounded the town of Field. Now just 100 kilometres from
home, the foursome began the last leg of the journey. They
reached Emerald Lake Road, near Field, after three days of
easy travel, then spent a little time cleaning themselves up.
Stains were removed from the women's riding skirts, shirts
were washed, newer shoes were pulled out of the duffel bags,
and shaving cream was applied on the men. When all were
sufficiently polished up, they took a moment to admire what
Mary called their "united elegance of appearance." Then they
headed to Field.

As they made their way to town, the outfit passed a lovely carriage going in the opposite direction. Suddenly, Mary
grew embarrassed at the thought of meeting up with
strangers. With her worn clothes and weather-beaten face,
she knew she looked nothing like a Philadelphia lady. What
would the travellers in the carriage think? Feeling ill at ease,
she bowed her head as the vehicle passed, but a furtive look
inside revealed a well-dressed couple staring back at her. The
carriage and its occupants passed quickly from Mary's
thoughts, and soon the foursome arrived in Field, where
friends were waiting to welcome them. In the buzz of
reunion, someone told Mary that the people in the carriage
were Mr. and Mrs. Rudyard Kipling, but Mary had other
things on her mind. Looking forward to the luxury of a bath,
a hard-boiled egg, and a nice dress, she left her faithful companions to seek out her rewards. Having just completed a

successful four-month expedition in the Canadian Rockies, she deserved them.

Chapter 8
Finding Chaba Imne

hen Mary Schäffer returned to Philadelphia in the fall of 1907, she brought many things home with her. She brought beautiful photographs and countless botanical specimens. She brought priceless memories of her days in the mountains and a diary filled with rollicking adventures. Most importantly, she brought home a crumpled piece of paper bearing a map to the mysterious Chaba Imne. Tucked between the pages of her diary, Sampson Beaver's map soon dominated Mary's thoughts, and she and Mollie began to plan another trip to the Canadian Rockies. Armed with the precious diagram, they would search for the secret lake that had eluded them that summer. And they would not quit until they found it.

Finding Chaba Imne

Billy Warren and Sid Unwin shared the women's desire to find Chaba Imne, and both men readily agreed to reprise their guiding roles. During the winter and spring of 1908, the four friends busied themselves with preparations for their upcoming summer. In the west, the men obtained the horses, got all the saddlery into shape, and fine-tuned the plans for another four-month trip. On the other side of the continent, Mary and Mollie gathered the food, clothing, and gear, making only a few changes to their packing list. This time, they bought waterproof bags for the food and regular canvas tents, avoiding the lightweight but flammable Egyptian sailcloth.

Mary also spent several hours preparing a miraculous camping food called pinole. Having learned the recipe from a seasoned camper, she roasted and ground countless cobs of corn into a fine flour. According to the camper, mixing a small portion of this flour with water provided a day's worth of sustenance. Covered in a fine dust of corn, Mary proudly surveyed the heaps of pinole she had prepared, happy in the knowledge that it would come to good use on the trail. (Little did she know that the grainy substance would taste and smell so awful that not even the horses would eat it.) She packed the pinole with the other gear and waited impatiently for the day when she could return to the Canadian Rockies.

Mary and Mollie arrived at Laggan on June 1, 1908. Once again, they were greeted by foul weather, but the group resolved that, come rain or shine, they would set out on June 8. This time, the group had grown. Two more eager explorers were joining Mary, Mollie, Billy, and Sid — botanist Stewardson Brown and his guide, Reggie Holmes. Brown, now working on a botanical project of his own, was excited to examine the flora of the regions Mary had enthusiastically told him about. Completing the expanded party was Sid Unwin's dog, Mr. Muggins, and 22 horses, 7 of which had been a part of the 1907 trip. Among the "old reliables" was Mary's faithful companion, Nibs.

Pelting rain fell non-stop for a solid week, but the group was determined. So on the morning of June 8, the new family set out for its latest adventure, traversing the same muskeg-covered trail that many of them had suffered through the summer before. The plan was to follow the Bow and North Saskatchewan Rivers to Nigel Creek, then to cross Nigel Pass and follow the Brazeau River to the mouth of Brazeau Lake. From there, the outfit would cross Poboktan Pass and begin the search for Chaba Imne. No one had any idea how long it would take to find the secret lake, but they had four whole months to find out.

Having got through their last expedition despite its many challenges, Mary and Mollie could not help but feel like wilderness pros. This time, they were confident enough to ride far ahead of their guides. Accompanying Brown, they made their way through muskeg and snow-laden grounds, getting themselves out of any jams they encountered. As they neared the North Saskatchewan, the women bombarded the botanist with stern warnings and friendly advice on how to handle crossing the river. Having experienced many harrowing river crossings, they wanted to share their hard-earned wisdom with their companion. But much to Mary's embarrassment, when it came time to cross the North Saskatchewan, the going was so easy that every member of the outfit made it across without the slightest incident. Days later, she was secretly vindicated when Brown and Billy had a terrible time fording the river after a side trip the two had made to the Kootenay Plains.

By the summer of 1908, Mary's confidence and enthusiasm had reached astonishing levels. No longer happy to stay put at camp while the men went off to explore, she eagerly joined them on hikes, climbs, and other excursions. This often meant leaving Mollie behind. Mollie, who was suffering from eye and heart trouble, didn't have the energy to join in activities that required physical exertion. Though Mary adored her friend, she simply could not be held back. There were too many things to see and collect and photograph, too many adventures to be had.

Some of Mary's excursions were filled with a little too much adventure. One afternoon, she accompanied Brown, Holmes, and Sid on a hike up the lower slopes of Mount Athabasca. The group spent much of the afternoon collecting fossils for Mollie. When they had accumulated about 25 kilograms' worth, all agreed it was time to return to the comfort of camp. However, thick patches of snow covered much of the mountainside, making the descent slick. While she managed to ease her way through some spots, Mary stopped cold when she came upon an especially long and icy patch — a patch that came to an end at a 15 metre precipice. Scared, she suggested that they find another way back, but Sid convinced his charge that if she followed in his tracks she would get down safely. Ever trusting of her guide, Mary obliged and carefully followed his trail. Holmes, who must have seen the fear in Mary's face, offered her his hand, and together the three made their way through the snow and ice. Suddenly, Holmes's feet shot out from under him. With a sickening yelp, he abandoned Mary's hand and went sliding toward the cliff, grabbing at snow and rocks in an effort to stop himself. The others watched in suspense as Holmes rolled toward the precipice, stopping on a pile of stones just short of the drop.

Relieved, Sid and Mary resumed their careful descent, but they had barely made any progress before Sid too lost his balance and slid down to the pile of rocks. Fighting back the urge to panic, Mary once again started her descent. But just as she resumed, Brown, who had been waiting at the top of the patch with every intention of sliding down it, let out a quick warning and glided by her on his bottom. He was received at the base of the patch with happy cheers and hearty laughter. As Mary continued to creep down the slope, she eyed her escorts, all three of whom were grinning up at her, helpless and amused. Realizing the ridiculousness of her fear, she let out a laugh then slid to the men on her backside.

Snow was a relentless obstacle in the quest for Chaba

Imne. Although it was summer, and many of the long days were filled with sunshine, plenty of snow still greeted the group along parts of the route. One of the most treacherous spots was Poboktan Pass. After having worked their way through burnt timber, muskeg, quicksand, and scree, the weary outfit reached Poboktan Pass only to discover that it was covered in deep snow. The winter conditions made horse feed scarce, and the horses were exhausted from slipping and sliding up and over the pass. Things got worse the second day, when the once well-marked trail ended abruptly. The guides spent a long time searching for the main trail, then gave up and led the party over an overgrown path for a few hours. According to Beaver's map, it appeared that they were travelling beyond their goal, but the day was waning and they had yet to find feed for the horses.

Finally, after more fruitless searching, the group came across an open stretch of land where they found sufficient feed, as well as abandoned teepee poles. The decision to stop for the night was a welcome one, but once camp was set up, everyone set off to investigate possible routes to the hidden lake. Awhile later, the party reconvened to report their findings. Only Billy had encouraging news — he had found the real Poboktan Pass, and the overgrown route they'd been taking would lead them to the true path. Although everyone was relieved that they could move forward in their search for the lake, the party was beginning to feel disheartened. So far, there had been no trace of Chaba Imne, and the weather was turning more dismal by the minute. That night, the wind blew with such vengeance that the tents and their contents threatened to depart into the valley below the camp.

The next morning was the fourth of July. Mary awoke to 15 centimetres of snow and bitterly cold weather reminiscent of the year before. In an effort to stay warm, the whole party piled into the women's tent to eat their breakfasts, but the bacon was "like candle grease, and the coffee barely warm." Despite the terrible weather, everyone agreed to push on, and with frozen fingers, they packed up camp and left the exposed area. For two hours, the guides chopped their way down a fire-swept valley, the rest of the contingent following sheepishly behind them. After a great deal of chopping, they reached a junction in the trail; one fork led to the valley of the Sunwapta River, and the other toward an opening in the hills to the north. Uncertain which trail to choose, members of the party debated the merits of each path. Some wanted to take the path to the Sunwapta, while others were certain the northern path would lead to the lake. In the end, the group took the northern path, struggling once more through biting winds and heavy snowdrifts. The way was getting increasingly difficult, and those who had wanted to take the trail to the Sunwapta were growing indignant. Finally, they decided to stop and set up camp.

The next morning, Billy and Sid went ahead to scout the terrain. They returned to camp late in the afternoon with news that there was another pass ahead but still no sign of

Chaba Imne. With wavering spirits, the group agreed they would push on in their search. But the newfound pass was just like the others — snowy. Once again the snow was heavy, and the horses stumbled through it at a snail's pace. When they finally got through the pass, a surprising sight greeted the group. Emerging from the fields of snow, they entered a beautiful valley that "swept away into an unbroken green carpet as far as the eye could see." Although they made their camp in the breathtaking green of the valley, the travellers had trouble enjoying their surroundings. Everyone's mind was on the elusive lake.

Discouraged, the gang sat down to lunch. As usual, they began to ponder the location of Chaba Imne and the accuracy of their route. Suddenly, Sid jumped up, shook himself, and said fiercely, "Well, it's two o'clock, but I'm going off to climb something that's high enough to see if that lake's within twenty miles of here, and I'm not coming back until I know!"

Mary desperately wanted to join Sid, but she knew he wouldn't appreciate anyone slowing him down. Instead, she waited with the others for his return. They filled much of the afternoon by looking for flowers and fossils and fighting off mosquitoes. When night fell and there was still no sign of Sid, the group began to worry. Donning their bug nets, they sat down to wait for their missing companion. Despite the heat of the night, they lit a bonfire, hoping it would be a useful marker. Finally, after eight and half hours away, Sid stumbled

Mary Schäffer

into camp looking worn out but pleased. Sitting down among his anxious friends, he announced happily, "I've found the lake!" Suddenly a great weight had been lifted. Everyone breathed a collective sigh of relief then listened as Sid described his gruelling journey. After climbing one ridge then hiking through a valley, he began to ascend another peak. When he reached the top, he looked out and there lay Chaba Imne, stretching out from a long valley below.

That night, Mary enjoyed a peaceful sleep, awakening the next morning to Billy shouting "All aboard for the lake!" After a quick breakfast, the revitalized explorers were on their way, excited to glimpse the water that had been eluding them for so long. Within two hours, they were standing on Chaba Imne's shores, awed by the lake's incredible beauty and humbled by the peacefulness of the scene before them.

Eager to explore the lake, the group found a suitable campsite a few kilometres from Maligne River, with plenty of feed nearby for the horses. The following day, the guides busied themselves with building a raft. The lake's shores were not horse-friendly, so the plan was to take three days' worth of food, along with tents and blankets, and sail to the head of the water. Mary watched as the guides built their boat. They worked quietly and efficiently; two men stood in the lake lashing logs together, while a third rolled trees toward them. By six o'clock that evening, the HMS *Chaba*, complete with upper and lower deck, was finished. It was scheduled to set sail for the upper end of the lake first thing in the morning.

Finding Chaba Imne

To Mary, the raft looked anything but reliable. It was "built without nail or spike, held together with wooden pegs and ropes," and it appeared to her that it would sink under too much weight. Not keen on having to swim in uncharted waters, Mary tried to think of ways to lighten the boat's load. She suggested leaving the air mattresses behind, but Billy and Sid vetoed the idea, insisting they would sail and camp in style. Having left the horses in the feed-filled campground, the guides began to load the raft. Mary watched with mounting anxiety as boxes and bundles were deposited on the upper deck. Minutes later, she tried to maintain some decorum as she too was carried out and dumped on board. Seated with Mollie atop blankets and bags of food, Mary was certain she would either sink or be tossed from her perch into the cold, green waters. But determined to be brave, she clutched a log and waited for disaster to strike.

As it turned out, the raft was surprisingly sturdy but "slow as a snail." The men took turns rowing the heavy load with two oversized sweeps. Listening to their laboured breathing, Mary wished there was some way she could help them. But since a woman would never be expected to row a raft carrying six people, a dog, and loads of gear, she sat back and enjoyed the lake's magnificent scenery. After a brief stop for lunch, the men continued to slowly manoeuvre the unlikely craft past breathtaking bays and inlets. Upon spotting the mountain from which Sid first saw the lake, the group christened it Mount Unwin. At about six thirty, the guides landed the raft near what they thought was the head of the lake and set up camp for the night.

The next day, the group resumed sailing, expecting to land shortly at the lake's head and climb its surrounding peaks. As they approached, Mary noticed that something was not right in Beaver's map. He had drawn narrows about two-thirds of the way down the lake, but these narrows had never appeared. Now nearing the water's end, Mary wondered how a map that had served them so well could be so glaringly wrong. But when they reached what they thought would be their debarking point, everything became clear: "There burst upon us that which, all in our little company agreed, was the finest view any of us had ever beheld in the Rockies ... miles and miles of lake, the unnamed peaks rising above us, one following the other, each more beautiful than the last. We had reached, not the end of the lake, but the narrows of which Sampson had told us."

The six companions spent the rest of the afternoon drinking in the view and naming many of the surrounding mountains. Over the course of the journey, they named Mount Warren, Mount Mary Vaux, the Thumb, and Sampson's Peak. The lake was so large that they spent all three of their allotted days rafting it, with no time left for climbing. There was time, however, to explore the shores at the lake's head, and, after a hearty lunch, Mary wandered around to take it all in. She later wrote, "How pure and undefiled it was! We searched for some sign that others had been there, — not a tepee pole, not a charred stick, not even tracks of game; just masses of flowers, the lap-lap of the waters on the shore, the occasional reverberating roar of an avalanche, and our own voices, stilled by a nameless Presence."

Mary had found what she'd been searching for: a perfect, pristine mountain paradise. When it came time to leave this paradise the next day, the friends reluctantly made their way to the raft. Before loading, Billy chopped a smooth surface on the side of a tree, and, for the first time in their travels, the group inscribed the date and their initials into the wood. As they sailed back to the horses, Mary and her companions took in the splendour of the lake and its mountains one last time. They landed at their original takeoff point at six o'clock, proud and certain that they had just completed the first ever voyage on what was soon to be known as Maligne Lake.

Now it was time to figure out how to spend the rest of the summer. With two months of exploring time remaining, Mary was eager to break more new ground. After some deliberation, the friends decided to head west to Mount Robson via the Yellowhead Trail. Not wanting to retrace their steps through the Maligne and Poboktan Passes, they took a shortcut by crossing the Maligne River heading northwest. To the naked eye, the river looked relatively harmless, but when Sid tried to cross it with his horse, a violent undertow nearly drowned both man and beast. Another try on a different horse led to two more near fatalities, and the group began to wonder if they should try a different route. However, after more attempts and the construction of another raft, the horses and their masters were able to cross the river safely. Unfortunately, five days of hard trail clearing along the Maligne River valley proved useless against the thick forests, and the party was eventually forced to return the way they came, through the Poboktan Valley to the Sunwapta River. From there they would head north to Mount Robson.

At the Sunwapta River, Brown and Holmes left the group to return to Laggan, taking nine horses with them. Mary, who had been suffering from terrible bouts of neuralgia from Maligne Lake to the Sunwapta, briefly considered returning with the botanist and his guide. But unwilling to give up her summer adventure so soon, she chose to keep travelling with Mollie, Sid, and Billy. The journey to Mount Robson was not an easy one, and though in terrible pain for much of it, Mary rode Nibs over logs and through muskeg, explored the Athabasca Valley, and even jumped down a canyon wall. Weeks later, her persistence was rewarded with the breathtaking view of the highest peak in the Canadian Rockies.

Still not ready to begin the journey home, the foursome considered stopping at Tête Jaune Cache, an historic site used long ago by a fair-haired Iroquois to stash his furs. In 1908, Tête Jaune Cache was the meeting point for prospectors, Native peoples, and surveyors of the Grand Trunk Pacific Railway. Mary had heard stories of the ruffians who visited the settlement, and though curious to see the historic cache, she and Mollie quietly feared they would be mugged or murdered by the thugs at the camp. As ever, Mary's curiosity got the better of her, and she decided she had to see Tête Jaune Cache. She rode into the tiny settlement with the rest of her party, her heart racing at the sight of the rough-looking men who watched her outfit pass by. Of this arrival Mary later wrote, "It seemed to me my hour had come. They looked awful and stood so terribly still as we slowly filed by them in the open. (It was only later that I wondered how much charity and faith might have been mustered on the spur of the moment to welcome us, and realised that we were probably quite as rough-looking in our travel-worn garments as those we rushed to condemn)."

Mary quickly realized that the men in Tête Jaune Cache were as harmless as Billy and Sid and even spent an afternoon visiting with the man who had frightened her the most upon her arrival. This man turned out to be Mr. Reading, a gentleman from Philadelphia, and the two Philadelphians discovered they had many friends in common. Before they parted ways, Mr. Reading requested that Mary and her party join the entire population of the town for dinner. As there were only three official residents at the time, this would by no means be a large dinner party. However, it was the first and only dinner party of the season for Mary and Mollie, and therefore it was an exciting invitation. The women dressed up as well as they could — Mollie tied a new leather shoestring in her hair, and Mary donned a new pair of moccasins and a pretty purple handkerchief. They felt distinctly dolled up and, upon arriving to dinner, took note that their men were clean-shaven and hatless.

But all formalities went out the window once dinner was served. Gobbling her delicious meal, Mary wondered what an outsider would have thought of her and her dinner companions. They ate in earnest, dispensing with unneeded plates and cutlery, and happily welcoming every bit of food they could fit in their stomachs. Far away from the refined city folk of the east, Mary and Mollie lost all sense of dining decorum, and each good-naturedly chided the other for her bad manners. Mary called attention to the fact that when asked if she wanted a second cup of tea, Mollie had gazed into her cup and tossed the cold tea on the floor. Mollie shot back that when the dessert was brought out, Mary had peered into the pot and asked in a most unladylike fashion, "What's this stuff?"

The dinner marked a wonderful end to the 1908 journey. Mary had again accomplished what she set out to do. Having found Chaba Imne, mastered muskeg and snow despite her painful neuralgia, and seen the tallest peak of the Canadian Rockies, she felt like a true adventurer. That night, after dinner, the companions drank a toast to meeting again in "civilized lands." Mary, however, wished those days would never come. She would later write a toast of her own: "Here's to a life of unnumbered summers in the mountains, with stars above by night, sunshine and soft winds by day, with the music of waters at our banquet." In her wanderings through the Canadian Rocky Mountains, Mary had truly grown to love "the free life of the trail."

Chapter 9

Changes

ary returned to Philadelphia in the fall of 1908 invigorated by her wilderness accomplishments. Immediately, she began searching for something new to feed her appetite for adventure. Soon enough she found what she was looking for: another trip. This time to Japan.

In the early 1900s, Asia was becoming an increasingly popular tourist destination for North Americans with money. Curious as to why, Mary read all she could about Japan and other Asian countries. She was inevitably captivated by this foreign place and grew keen to learn first-hand about its history, its flora, and its people. By late fall 1908, she and Mollie

Changes

Adams, along with two other lady friends, were ready to set off on an eastern adventure.

Mary's trip to Japan was crammed with activity. Upon her arrival, she made it clear that while she wanted to see the usual tourist attractions of central and southern Japan, she also wanted to see the country's lesser-known features, including the northern territory of the aboriginal Ainu. Similar to her earlier fixation with the Native peoples of North America, Mary was eager to observe and somehow connect with the Ainu. At first she had difficulty finding anyone willing to escort her, but she managed to secure the services of a like-minded Japanese guide. Together, they set off to the village of Piratori, travelling by boat, train, and horse-drawn cart. After taking many photographs of the Ainu and observing their ways of life up close, Mary returned to her friends, pleased that she'd been able to experience a bit of Japan's aboriginal culture.

Later in the trip, Mary and her companions were escorted to Taiwan, where an excited Mary caught a glimpse of the culture of the Formosan headhunters. The women stayed in Taiwan for Christmas and New Year's and enjoyed a distinctly foreign holiday, replete with a 22-course Chinese dinner. Not wanting to miss out on a thing, Mary tried all 22 courses, including shark's fins and pigeon's eggs. Unfortunately, Mollie contracted pneumonia while in Taiwan, and her condition worsened as the women prepared to leave the island. Sadly, Mollie Adams, Mary's treasured friend and travel companion, died on the boat ride back to Japan. She was buried in Kobe.

Heartbroken by Mollie's death, Mary returned to Philadelphia, where she was forced once again to find ways in which to deal with her grief. Not ready to escape to the Canadian Rockies, she honoured her friend by telling tales of their adventures to others. Sharing her stories was not a new pursuit for Mary. She had been writing about her mountain travels for several years, penning articles for newspapers, magazines, and scientific journals. Her enthusiasm for the Canadian Rockies was so great that she felt compelled to pass it on. In fact, she made it somewhat of a personal vocation to convert others to a love of the great outdoors. Her writings were often directed at women readers, for she wanted other women to experience the joys of the mountains. In a self-admonishing way, Mary insisted that if she was able to ride on rough terrain or explore a deep cave, so could they.

Aware that her exploits were of interest to others, and wanting to work on something of value after Mollie's death, Mary decided to write a book-length account of their 1907 and 1908 adventures. She was soon reminded that work was the perfect panacea. Drawing mostly from the diaries she and Mollie had kept, as well as from her memory and the extensive knowledge of Tom Wilson, Mary spent almost two years writing a magical travel narrative. The result was *Old Indian Trails in the Canadian Rockies*, published in 1911 by G. P. Putnam's Sons. Dedicated to Mollie, the book received excellent reviews, furthering Mary's reputation as both a wilderness expert and an intriguing adventurer. A reviewer for the *New York Times* wrote: "In reading *Old Indian Trails* by Mary Schäffer, it is difficult to decide just what impresses us most: the excellence of the writing, the picturesqueness of the country described, or the personality of the author herself."

The year 1911 was an eventful one for Mary. Only months before her book was to hit bookstores, she received an appealing offer. A friend, Dr. D. B. Dowling of the Geological Survey of Canada, asked if she would be willing to survey and map Maligne Lake. Until 1908, the lake had been among the best-kept secrets of the Canadian Rockies. The only people who had known of its whereabouts were native hunters and one lonely CPR surveyor who had happened upon it in 1875. After Mary and her companions "rediscovered" the lake and its surrounding peaks, interest in the area grew. Believing that a survey would be valuable, Dowling knew that Mary was the ideal person to carry out the task. Not only would she be a capable and reliable worker, her own increasing fame would certainly help promote the beauty of the newly formed Jasper Park, where Maligne Lake is situated.

Taking his idea to the commissioner of parks in Edmonton, Dowling soon received funding to cut a trail to the lake. He then spent time convincing Mary that she was the right person for the job. Although she had no experience as a surveyor, Dowling assured his wary friend that he could teach her the necessary skills. With that promise, and the prospect of seeing the lake again, the offer was too good to pass up. That May, along with her sister-in-law, Caroline Sharpless, and her eight-year-old nephew, Paul, Mary returned to the mountains she loved so dearly.

Mary's second journey to Maligne Lake was nothing like her first. Since 1908, the march of progress had made its indelible mark on the Canadian mountain wilderness. Construction of a second transcontinental railway, the Grand Trunk Pacific, was well under way through Yellowhead Pass. For the first time, Mary reached her mountain playground via this northern route. After several stopovers, she and her travelling companions arrived in Prairie Creek, a construction settlement several kilometres north of their true destination. From there, Mary, Caroline, and Paul reached Maligne Lake on horseback. This time, however, the trail was cut out ahead of them, and they reached the lake with relative ease.

Guided by Sid Unwin and Jack Otto, the travellers had a wonderful time camping, and the worries of the trail were comparatively few. Even fording the Athabasca River was easier; at one of its crossing points, a ferry, complete with a toll, now carried wary travellers and horses across the water's depths. Amazed by the new and simple route to the lake, Mary was learning "by experience the difference between entering a country locked away from the world, and the same one when the door was swinging wide open for the first time." In 1908, it had taken Mary's party almost a month to reach Maligne Lake. This time, it took eight days.

Changes

Despite the differences between trips past and present, one thing remained the same for Mary: the lake was still absolutely breathtaking. Upon reaching its shores, the guides set to work building a large boat, constructed not out of logs, ropes, and pegs, but of lumber that had been carried on horseback. When the HMS *Chaba II* was completed, Mary wasted no time in getting down to work, completing an accurate survey of Maligne Lake in just over a month. Though proud of her accomplishment, she was sad to leave her beloved lake behind, knowing that encroaching development would soon change the view before her forever.

Having completed her assignment for Dowling, Mary was not ready to return to Philadelphia. After saying goodbye to Caroline and Paul in Edmonton, she made her way to Banff, where she spent the fall season in a rented cottage. There, she visited with many friends and observed the town's off-season hum. Tired of city life and longing for a change, Mary had begun to wonder if she should move to Banff permanently. Having never truly embraced the social life of upper-middle class Philadelphia, Mary had few reasons to continue living there. Her parents and husband were long gone, and her brothers were always travelling. Though she had other relatives and friends in the city, she felt much closer to her peers in the Rockies. The only thing holding Mary back from a move to Banff was her belief that the harsh Canadian winters would be too much for her to handle. To test herself, she decided to spend the winter of 1912 in her favourite mountain town. Much to her delight, the weather proved tolerable, and her winter stay was a success. As a result, at the age of 51, Mary decided it was time to make a permanent move west. Returning to Philadelphia to prepare, she asked Billy Warren to find her a nice lot in town.

Several months later, with her bags packed and her crated furniture headed west, Mary could hardly wait to see what her trusted guide had found. Billy had conveyed that he was pleased with his find, and Mary pictured a perfect property, overlooking valleys and peaks and the charms of the town. When she saw the actual lot, she could barely contain her disappointment — it was directly across from the Banff cemetery. Knowing that Billy had done his best and not wanting to hurt his feelings, Mary gladly accepted the property. She built a modest home and settled into her new house quickly, decorating it with many furnishings from Philadelphia, as well as native artifacts she had collected over the years. She named her home Tarry-a-While and opened it up to friends and visitors.

One of Mary's closest friends in Banff was Billy Warren. Since her first tenderfoot trips with him in 1904, she had grown increasingly fond of her guide, developing a deep respect for his ability and his kindness. Billy, in return, held a great admiration for Mary, and in time the two fell in love. In 1915, Mary Schäffer married Billy Warren, who was 19 years her junior. She was devoted to her husband, and with her support — both emotional and financial — he became a prominent businessman in Banff.

Changes

While Billy was working, Mary spent time writing and volunteering for organizations in town. During World War I, she also helped with the war effort on the home front, sending a set of her hand-coloured lantern slides of the Canadian Rockies to wounded soldiers in English hospitals. Since her first major expedition in 1907, Mary had devoted many spring and winter days to giving lantern slide shows, enticing audiences all over North America with her fascinating mountain tales and wilderness tips. The slides she sent overseas had their desired effect: they entertained the wounded and brought parts of home to Alberta soldiers overseas. Mary's help with the war effort was partly fuelled by her own personal interest — her nephew, Eric, and good friend Sid Unwin were both killed in battle. In her grief, Mary oversaw the creation of a memorial to Banff's war dead, a memorial that still stands in front of the Legion on Banff Avenue.

During her years in Banff, Mary became one of the town's most active and well-known residents. She had many friends in the community, and her door was always open to them. People of all ages were drawn to Mary's enthusiasm, but she herself preferred the younger generation. Happy to be connected to the hopeful, energetic pulse of youth, she often hosted dinner parties and card games for the town's young adults. Tarry-a-While was also a draw for younger children, who visited Mary's house to get a glimpse of the monkey and parrot she kept as pets.

Eventually, Mary's health deteriorated. After a number of falls and an automobile accident, she grew increasingly weak and unwell. Around the same time, Billy started to experience serious heart trouble, and his wife's mental and physical well-being suffered all the more. Mary Schäffer Warren died of pneumonia on January 23, 1939, at the age of 77. Billy Warren died four years later. They are buried together in the cemetery across from their home, embraced by the mountains that Mary loved so much.

Mary Schäffer Warren led an extraordinary life. Through sheer determination, she overcame hardships and fears, developing a sense of adventure that ultimately knew no bounds. She challenged the rules and restrictions of her day and consequently opened doors for countless female travellers. Mary was a woman ahead of her time. A daring explorer, her love of the Canadian Rockies was all-encompassing and utterly infectious. Her remarkable accomplishments have inspired, and continue to inspire, men and women of all ages, in all walks of life.

Bibliography

Adams, Mary. Trip Diary. Banff, AB: Archives of the Canadian Rockies, M79: 10.

Beck, Janice Sanford. *No Ordinary Woman: The Story of Mary Schäffer Warren*. Calgary: Rocky Mountain Books, 2001.

Hart, E. J. *Diamond Hitch*. Banff: Summerthought, 1979.

Hart, E. J, ed. *A Hunter of Peace*. Banff: Whyte Museum of the Canadian Rockies, 1980.

Hart, E. J. *Jimmy Simpson: Legend of the Rockies*. Banff: Altitude Publishing, 1991.

Hart, E. J. *The Place of Bows*. Banff: EJH Enterprises Ltd., 1999.

Love, Currie. "Pushing Ahead of Trails." *Canada West Monthly* (August 1911): 273–9.

Schäffer, Mary. "The Heart of a Child." Banff, AB: Archives of the Canadian Rockies, M79: 7.

Schäffer, Mary. "My Garden." Banff, AB: Archives of the Canadian Rockies, M79: 2.

Schäffer, Mary. "The Story of Revelstoke." Banff, AB: Archives of the Canadian Rockies, M79: 6.

Schäffer, Mary. "Tepee Life in the Northern Hills." Banff, AB: Archives of the Canadian Rockies, M79: 6.

Schäffer, Mary T. S. "Untrodden Ways." *Canadian Alpine Journal* 1:2 (1908) 288–94.

Smith, Cyndi. *Off the Beaten Track.* Jasper: Coyote Books, 1989.

Warren, Mary S. "In the Heart of the Canadian Rockies with Horse and Camera. Part I." Banff, AB: Archives of the Canadian Rockies, M189: 7.

Warren, Mary S. "In the Heart of the Canadian Rockies, Part II." Banff, AB: Archives of the Canadian Rockies, M189: 7.

About the Author

Jill Foran lives and writes in Calgary, Alberta. Specializing in personal and company histories, she has written profiles, biographies, and memoirs for magazine and book publishers and corporations. She has also written more than 30 non-fiction books for children.

Acknowledgments

The author wishes to acknowledge Mary Schäffer's published and unpublished manuscripts for the quotes in this manuscript. All photographs are courtesy of the Whyte Museum.

OTHER AMAZING STORIES

These titles are available wherever you buy books. Visit our Web site at **www.amazingstories.ca**

New **AMAZING STORIES®** titles are published every month.